Y0-BDK-237

GOD IN THE
LABORATORY

2017
DF

W
50
.T78
2000

GOD IN THE LABORATORY

EQUIPPING CHRISTIANS TO DEAL WITH ISSUES IN BIOETHICS

AL TRUESDALE

Beacon Hill Press of Kansas City
Kansas City, Missouri

Copyright 2000
by Beacon Hill Press of Kansas City

ISBN 083-411-7932

Printed in the
United States of America

Cover Design: Paul Franitza

All Scripture quotations not otherwise designated are from the
Holy Bible, New International Version® (NIV®). Copyright © 1973,
1978, 1984 by International Bible Society. Used by permission of
Zondervan Publishing House. All rights reserved.

Permission to quote from the following additional copyrighted ver-
sions of the Bible is acknowledged with appreciation:

Contemporary English Version (CEV). Copyright © by American
Bible Society, 1991, 1992.

New Revised Standard Version (NRSV) of the Bible, copyright 1989
by the Division of Christian Education of the National Council of
the Churches of Christ in the USA. All rights reserved.

Revised Standard Version (RSV) of the Bible, copyright 1946, 1952,
1971 by the Division of Christian Education of the National Council
of the Churches of Christ in the USA.

Scripture quotations marked KJV are from the King James Version.

10   9   8   7   6   5   4   3   2   1

For Esther

CONTENTS

ACKNOWLEDGMENTS

I want to express my gratitude to Donna Techau and Leslie Brown for their research assistance. I also express appreciation to Bonnie Perry and Shannon Hill of Beacon Hill Press of Kansas City for their patience and excellent counsel during the production of *God in the Laboratory*.

INTRODUCTION

Isn't it exciting to embrace a new century and a new millennium? There are many reasons to be wide-eyed with anticipation over what the future holds. When the 20th century opened, some brave souls dared to predict that in that century we would learn to fly like the birds. As the 21st century opens, scientists are beginning to translate photography used in spacecraft into a technique for early detection of breast cancer. By the time this century ends, people will probably look back with amusement on some of our "cutting-edge breakthroughs." Given the speed at which technology changes, we won't have to wait long to revise some of our expectations.

We're living in an age of questions. How will the earth's resources be divided among the nations? What surprises await us in the development and utilization of technology? How will information be gathered and distributed? What modifications will occur in social organization? How will education change?

To what distant places in the universe will persons freely travel? How many of the current diseases will we file away as social and medical history? In what new and changed environments will persons live and play? Will ethnic groups within countries that have been in conflict for generations learn to live in peace? Will technological, social, and philosophical developments change the way we define "person"?

Whatever the answers are to these questions, we will grow accustomed to living in a postmodern world, the "modern era" having now become one we study in World History 101. Creatively responding to the challenges and opportunities we will meet in the global village will require our best and most imaginative energies.

How will the Church of Jesus Christ greet this new

century and millennium? As in the past, the responses
will be broadly diverse. From the beginning, Christians
have given divergent appraisals of the world and their role
in it. Confronted by increasing religious pluralism, for example, some Christians will circle the wagons ever more
tightly, hoping to stave off the enemy until help comes
from on high. Others will so freely mix the Christian story
with the stories of other religions, worldviews, and values
that their distinction as Christians will largely disappear.
But thoughtful, responsible Christians will see the need to
look carefully at the social, political, and technological
challenges a new century brings. They will search for creative ways to maintain the integrity of the Christian faith
while engaging in culture in its many forms.

To learn how to faithfully articulate and embody the
Christian story in all dimensions of life and human responsibility, we carefully use all the Christian resources
available to us, including Scripture, tradition, reason, and
experience. In many instances, answers to questions and
the directions a Christian should take will be explicit and
clear. At other points, Christians will have to make decisions for which neither the Scriptures nor Christian tradition provide precise guidance. However, there will be no
reason to fear, for having learned in community the Christian story, we'll be able to go on from here. Living under
the Holy Spirit's guidance and being nurtured in the
Church, we will have the experience to complete the
Christian melody even when sections of the score have
not been written.

Richard Middleton and Brian Walsh speak of how important it is for Christians to "indwell the Christian drama by serious, passionate study of the Scriptures" until
the character of the Christian drama becomes our character. If this happens, then we can be confident that the
Spirit will teach us how to be "faithful to the thrust, mo-
mentum and direction of the biblical story."[1]

Bioethics is one of the major realms in which Christians must be equipped to live effectively. The Holy Spirit will tell the story through the lives of faithful believers, in their values, and by the decisions they make.

What Is Bioethics?

"Bioethics" is composed of two Greek words: *bios* (life) and *ethike* (ethics). Warren Reich in *The Encyclopedia of Bioethics* says that bioethics is "the systematic study of the moral dimensions—including moral vision, decisions, conduct, and policies—of the life sciences and health care. Bioethics uses a variety of ethical methodologies in an interdisciplinary setting."[2] The moral dimensions that bioethics examines tend to focus on several major questions: "What is a person's (or a society's) moral vision? What sort of person should one be? What ought to be done in specific situations? And how are we to live harmoniously?"[3] Bioethicist Thomas A. Shannon says, "Bioethics examines the ethical dimensions of problems at both the heart and the cutting edge of technology, medicine, and biology in their application to life."[4] In another definition, we learn that bioethics is the field of theoretical and applied ethics that critically examines the moral dimensions of biotechnical and biomedical technology and decision-making in health-related contexts and in contexts involving the biological sciences. Bioethics includes what used to be called "medical ethics."

Tom L. Beauchamp and James F. Childress use "biomedical ethics" as a synonym for "bioethics."[5] By either name, bioethics is the discipline that deals with the moral implications of both biological research and the applications of that research, especially in medicine. Widely disciplinary, bioethics draws upon medicine, jurisprudence, civil government, economics, theology, philosophy, psychology, sociology, industry, and biology.

Bioethics as we know it today is of fairly recent origin. But its roots reach all the way back to ancient times. The famous oath of Hippocrates (5th century B.C.), for example, dealt with the ethics of medical care given by a physician. That topic remains an important part of bioethics. From the days of Hippocrates until the 1950s, the standards of medical ethics were fairly uniform. Then the "long-standing traditions began to be supplanted, or at least supplemented."[6] In the middle of the 20th century we witnessed the large-scale appearance of biotechnology. There were significant changes in health care, advances in the biological sciences, and acute problems relating to the distribution of scarce medical resources. New questions arose that made "medical ethics" too narrow a category for naming the constellation of topics that now compose bioethics.

During the second half of the 20th century, public awareness and interest in bioethics intensified, largely because of new possibilities in such concerns as assisted reproductive technologies and genetic engineering. As biotechnical developments expanded, the media showed an increased interest in bioethics. The impossible became commonplace, and people eagerly began to read about and discuss the implications of what was previously regarded as esoteric biomedical research. Many became familiar with the importance of DNA (deoxyribonucleic acid) and its primary structure even if they did not understand the details. By expanding the realm of public discourse, bioethics has drawn the sciences and the humanities, philosophy and theology, jurisprudence and politics, psychology and sociology into the discussion.

The subjects normally treated by bioethics are fairly standard: moral constraints upon technology; just access to health care; patients' rights (such as autonomy, nonmaleficence, and justice); the professional/ethical responsibilities of medical professionals (relationships between health-care providers and those in their care); the right to refuse medical treatment; abortion; defining death, euthanasia, and the right to die; distribution of scarce medical resources (including transplantation); the ethics of experimentation; genetic intervention (genetic testing, screening, and engineering); reproductive technologies (including the prospects of human cloning); and genetic engineering in agriculture.

Four basic principles of medical ethics are widely accepted today. As we proceed, we need to be aware of them. The first is *beneficence,* the duty to do good for one's patients. The second is closely aligned with the first: *nonmaleficence,* to do no harm. The third principle is *autonomy,* the patient's right to self-determination. The fourth is *justice,* the attempt to be fair, to treat people with reasonable equity, establishing goals and criteria for medicine and research that do not discriminate against persons on the basis of religion, gender, race, and so forth.[7]

In this book we will not have reason to discuss the role of bioethics committees. But their existence and importance should be noted briefly. Numerous groups are involved in setting policy and making decisions in bioethics: (1) bioethics research institutes, or "think tanks," such as the Hastings Center and the Kennedy Institute of Ethics (over 200 such centers exist throughout the world);[8] (2) centers, such as the Midwest Bioethics Center in Kansas City, that are principally concerned with applied bioethics; (3) major United States presidential commissions, which focus on policies that apply across institutions; (4) ethics committees, created principally by institutions such as hospitals. An institution's administration or medical staff establishes the committees' legal or bureaucratic authority. The task of a bioethics committee is to assist in making difficult bioethical decisions; their ultimate responsibility is to the patients. Bioethics committees are common in major hospitals.[9]

Changes in Health Care—Moral Implications

The 20th century witnessed an unprecedented revolution in medicine and health care. At its beginning, little could be done for the victims of most infectious organisms. In the case of local infections, doctors could not go beyond drainage, poultices, and ointments. For severe diseases, doctors could prescribe only rest and nourishment. By current standards, the hopes of medical professionals were modest. They dreamed of having vaccines and chemical remedies.

As the century's medical and biotechnical revolution advanced, the general population benefited, mostly in the developed countries. In 1901, life expectancy was 48 years for males and 51.6 years for females in the United Kingdom. By the 1980s it had reached 71.4 years for males and 77.2 years for females. Other industrialized nations showed similar dramatic increases. No one in his or her wildest dreams could have predicted that by the end of the 20th century researchers would have understood and even taken early steps to manipulate the basic building blocks of organisms. In 1953 British biophysicist Francis H. C. Crick and United States biochemist James Watson, using data obtained by Maurice Wilkins at King's College, London, discovered the molecular structure of deoxyribonucleic acid (DNA), the chemical substance ultimately responsible for hereditary control of life functions. Then, by the close of the century, researchers astonished the world by isolating and successfully culturing the first human pluripotent stem cell lines. Biomedical research moved toward a new and extraordinarily promising frontier.

Early in the 21st century, 100 percent of the human genome (the sum total of all human genes) was mapped and sequenced. A subsequent step will be to provide DNA chips that analyze one's personal genetic makeup.[10] Doctors will be able to consult a person's genetic profile in order to design therapies. Using knowledge already gained from gene mapping, researchers even now are pursuing control of the aging process itself. In 1999 Italian scientists extended the life span of mice up to 35 percent by breeding them without a gene that produces a protein vulnerable to cell oxidation—the process we call "aging."

But such anticipated and realized biomedical advances usually arrive attached to moral and social questions. While technology is theoretically a morally neutral entity, we know that the real-life dilemmas caused by technology are anything but morally neutral. Commenting in *Cruzan v. Missouri Department of Health (1990)*, Justice Antonin Scalia, Justice of the Supreme Court of the United States, spoke of "the constantly increasing power of science to keep the human body alive for longer than any reasonable person would want to inhabit it."[11] Technology is often put to uses that raise moral questions of serious individual and societal importance. The introduction of nuclear energy in the last century serves as a good example. After some notable near disasters, the use of nuclear energy generated intense moral debate. Similarly, introducing new biotechnical applications into health-related contexts often generates moral and social apprehension. Sustained debates about what is right, humane, and just often result.

Conflict between technological promise and moral danger is sometimes referred to as "the Daedalus effect." Daedalus was a legendary figure of classical mythology— a craftsman, inventor, architect, and artist. He generated ideas and solved problems. However, each question he answered raised several more, and each problem he solved led to new ones. His creations brought with them both positive and negative consequences.

Much like Daedalus's inventions, revolutionary medical treatment, new diagnostic techniques, and public health measures nearly always raise new questions and spark debate. Christians should not think that by simplistic appeal to a Bible verse or the tenets of Christian tradition they can escape all the tensions and dilemmas that others face. It is simply the case that biomedical developments often occur that outstrip the supply of answers we

already have in hand. For example, when the DNA chips
that will analyze a person's genetic makeup become
available, who should have access to such vital and comprehensive information? The chip will eventually provide
predictions regarding the diseases for which a person is
at risk. Should one's employer or insurer have access to
the information? One's prospective spouse? Or should it
be the property of the individual only? The Church must
help Christians learn how to analyze moral complexity
when it exists, how to make use of biotechnology, and
how to make decisions in ways that are consistent with
the content of their faith.

Bioethics and the Christian

Many developments occur in science that don't immediately affect the daily lives of most citizens. So while
they're interesting, they're of no urgent moral or religious
significance. For example, how gravity made galaxies out
of atoms long after God brought the universe into being is
an immensely intriguing story. Such secrets of the universe are very important for understanding God's majes-
tic world.[12] But for most of us, such information will never
be as urgent as our access to adequate health care or our
decision to use costly reproductive technology. Bioethical
advances impose such questions on us. But while technology can prompt the questions, it cannot by itself answer them. For that task we turn to religious and moral
resources. Left to technological answers alone, we could
not fulfill the meaning of being human.

At some point in our lives or those of family members, most of us will have to make difficult moral decisions regarding bioethical issues. If an initial sense of
panic grips us, we should not be surprised. One of the by-
products of the astonishing successes in biomedicine is
that often the increase in technological options compli-
cates the existing scenario. Without warning, we may be
called upon to make decisions for which we're neither

technically, experientially, nor morally prepared.
We can no more escape the promises and problems
generated by health-related technology than we can escape our responsibilities as parents, as custodians of elderly parents, or as citizens. Without our even knowing
much about the term, "bioethics" has become a part of
our lives. Christian health-care professionals are directly
involved on a regular basis, as are research scientists, at-
torneys, educators, and legislators. Chaplains and parish
ministers are also included.[13] Resolving problems in ways
that are faithful to the Christian story will require freedom to think and act in accordance with Christian principles and virtues.

As Christians, we face the danger that our moral responses to biotechnology will not be distinctively Christian. Additionally, while being morally defensible, we may
find ourselves in the uncomfortable position of adopting a
posture that is little more than a secular ethic tinged with
a religious flavor, not at all grounded in and informed by
the faith we confess. This challenge for Christians is more
difficult because bioethical issues arise and are defined
without any necessary reference to Christian faith.

In science the questions are technical and not religious in nature.[14] They arise in a pluralistic and secular
world where no single religion, including Christianity,
provides normative answers.

The standard by which we ought to be judged is not
by how successfully we address a pluralistic society, but
by how coherently we apply Christian convictions to
questions raised in the ever-expanding applications of
biotechnology. James Gustafson sums it up well: "[All of
us] must help Christians understand technology in the
light of their religious faith and convictions."[15]

PART 1

Christian Beliefs and Bioethics

While the term "bioethics" has a fairly uniform definition, the moral visions or structures that persons use for making bioethical decisions are quite diverse. The principles a bioethicist uses to offer moral guidance with reference to euthanasia, for example, will depend upon the moral framework within which he or she functions. This moral framework may rest upon religious foundations, or it may not.[1]

Utilitarianism (also called *consequentialism*) is one model for decision making that rests on a nonreligious foundation. Persons who function as utilitarian will choose a course of action that promises to achieve the greatest amount of value. Utilitarianism need have no relationship with religion. Another option in moral theory that does not require religious foundations is *deontological ethics,* which looks to one's duty to moral law, *deon,* or to what he or she "knows" to be right. *Rights ethics* holds that moral problems are resolved in terms of a hierarchy of rights that are intrinsic and not arbitrary. *Intuition* solves moral problems by deciding the right and the wrong on the power of one's moral faculty. In *virtue theory* a person makes decisions according to a set of internalized virtues that shape his or her character.

If one chooses to make bioethical decisions from within a religious framework, then the decisions should evidence the defining center of that religion. So if a rabbi were to give counsel to a wife and husband regarding reproductive technology, we would expect the counsel to be guided by the defining convictions of Judaism. When Christians seek answers to moral questions, they should examine the principal resources that inform their faith. They should make decisions that express the substance of the Christian faith and their convictions regarding its truthfulness. These decisions should express belief in Jesus Christ as the One in whom God has revealed himself and His will for creation. The Christian ethic expresses a confidence that in Christ, God revealed the truth about human life.

Let's examine some of the important Christian beliefs that should guide us when we face tough moral decisions.

1

BIOETHICS: CHALLENGE AND OPPORTUNITY FOR THE CHURCH

The importance of the Church in all of this cannot be overestimated. The whole story of God should shape us as persons. With reference to bioethics, the Church has a responsibility to study and live the Scriptures and to learn the mind of the Holy Spirit. Together, we as members of Christ's body can learn how to make bioethical decisions for ourselves and to offer guidance to others. While few persons have the need to develop expertise in bioethics, most of us will be called upon at some time to decide and act as moderately informed persons.

Christians everywhere live in cultures that make legitimate social and economic claims upon them, as is true for their non-Christian neighbors. But unlike any human institution, the Church is a countercultural community of discipleship. The Church has been and continues to be addressed by God. Here God forms a covenant people whose lives are to bear the impress, the very character, of God. "The primary sphere of moral concern is not the character of the individual but the corporate obedience of the Church."[1]

Christians should never have to become moral and religious "lone rangers," applying their faith as isolated units. Rather, we learn the Christian faith and its ethic in community, in the Body of Christ. The Church must provide a zone of safety where infertile Christian couples will be free to express their pain. There the husband of a terminally ill wife can freely express his agony over whether to continue life-support measures. In the Church believers should help each other acquire those virtues that will equip them for witness to the values they embrace and the decisions they make.

All of us will need just such a community, for the world of bioethics challenges many traditional ideas that Christians have held regarding life and death, justice and health. Faithfulness to the gospel of our Lord, to the Scriptures, and to the demands of life leaves no place for insensitivity or superficiality.

In some cases the Christian answers to bioethical questions are clear-cut. In other instances the answers are not so simple, but we must seek God's guidance for the journey. We must rest on the conviction that the Christian life is one of grace. We are reconciled to God by grace and faith alone, not by human accomplishments or human perfection. The gracious God holds us to himself even when the ideal is not within our reach, when we are vulnerable and confused.

Bioethics also presents an opportunity to demonstrate the vitality and range of our faith, and its moral substance. The Church in this age has a unique opportunity, as did first-century Christians, to show how the Christian faith imparts a quality and meaning to life and death that can come only from the One who was dead and is now alive forevermore.

The Bible and Christian Ethics

When inquiring about morality, the Christian should turn primarily to the Bible. Historically, Protestant churches have affirmed that the Old and New Testaments were given by divine inspiration and that they faithfully reveal God's will concerning all things necessary to salvation and to the practice of Christian discipleship.

The Bible bears witness to God, not to itself. God is its subject—God in covenant with humanity. It tells the marvelously varied yet united story of how God brought into existence both the world and a people. It tells of God's choosing to be with us and of His being with us as a faithful covenantal partner. The story of the Bible is one of grace. It tells how a holy God freely gives himself to His creation, how that even when people failed to maintain covenant with Him, He just kept on coming, seeking reconciliation. The Bible tells how the eternal God became incarnate, one with us in Jesus of Nazareth. It tells the good news of how God took upon himself the sin of the world and did for us what we absolutely could not do for ourselves.

The story of God is also the story of Christ's Church, His body. In fact, the Church is to be the embodied story of God. Those who are its many members have one defining reason for being: to tell, to embody the story of God. Essentially, the Christian ethic is quite simple. It is the empowered mode of life in which the name of God is declared in all the earth.

So the primary significance of the Bible is that it makes known a holy God who is Creator and Redeemer and who has acted decisively to reconcile the world to himself. Nothing else in the Bible should be allowed to take the place of this central significance.

Today we are confronted by bioethical questions that our forefathers did not face. Whether or not to remove a breathing tube from the trachea of a cancerous husband involves a moral predicament the apostle Paul obviously did not confront. Written before people even knew about the circulatory system, the Bible should not be expected to answer questions its writers could not have anticipated. The proper use of the Bible in the life of the Church is not to treat it as an exhaustless catalog of questions and answers but to find there those resources that will develop the virtues that mark us as true children of God.

The Bible does not imperialistically silence the contributions that science, reason, and philosophy make to human understanding. Instead, it provides the criteria for determining the role of these other resources. When we use other disciplines to help us make informed decisions, we are not diminishing the Bible's importance. Instead, we are showing that we recognize its centrality. We demonstrate that God is present in all creation and uses it to manifest His name.

The Bible is most instructive not as a catalog of answers to all moral questions but as the *primary source* for learning about God and His relationship to humanity and to the rest of creation. By listening carefully to God's Word and being transformed by Him, we form virtues that reflect the character of God and that help us think and act in ways that are distinctively Christian.

Christian Ethics and Bioethics

The Gospel of Mark tells us that after John the Baptist was arrested, "Jesus came into Galilee, preaching the gospel of God, and saying, 'The time is fulfilled, and the kingdom of God is at hand; repent, and believe in the gospel'" (Mark 1:14-15, RSV). The gospel that Christians receive by grace through faith, which makes them new creatures in Christ, is the good news of God. And it's news about the kingdom of God, for the gospel is the "gospel of the kingdom of God."

The good news is that in Jesus of Nazareth, the long-expected kingdom of God—the reign of God—has come to earth. God extends His grace to all. In the person of Christ, God gives himself to all persons who will receive Him. The people who had no hope based on their own merits and religious status heard Jesus gladly. In Him they saw and heard the news that the old order of enslavement to sin had been broken—and could be broken in them. They heard from Jesus a gospel that makes all things new (2 Cor. 5:14-21). Those who heard Jesus, who repented of their sins and received the good news, were "born anew"; they were "born from above." The old passed away; the new came. It was nothing less than a

new creation, a *new way of being* given by the gracious
God.

Out of the new way of being, the new life of victori-
ous grace, there arose a *new way of doing*. The Christian
ethic is not just rooted in the gospel of the Kingdom but
expresses, replicates in human life, the gospel. The Christian ethic has nothing at all to do with carrying a heavy
load of legal demands. Quite the contrary, it is the "law of
freedom." "For freedom . . . Christ has set us free," Paul
told the Galatian Christians (Gal. 5:1).

Let us be clear—the Christian ethic is an ethic of the
grace of Christ, of the indwelling Spirit who concretely
forms us, in community, into the image of Christ. In all of
the moral dimensions of life Christians should seek to follow this pattern. This includes a realm as potentially
thorny as bioethics. When Christians deal with bioethics,
they have one responsibility: to choose the course of action
that will best manifest the gospel of the kingdom of God.

None of us should ever be left alone to do all of this
by ourselves. The Christian ethic is the ethic of *koinonia,*
the Church, the fellowship of the Holy Spirit. It is in the
Body of Christ that we gain strength, wisdom, encourage-
ment, and forgiveness.

The Christian ethic is a "can-do" ethic. It is the ethic
of the good news that sets us free. Christ sets us free
from the law of sin and death. He sets us free *for himself,
for our neighbor, for the world as His creation,* and *for
ourselves as centers of legitimate value.*

The Christian ethic is also a redemptive ethic. It
breathes life and hope, not condemnation and oppression. When Jesus gave instructions regarding ethics, He
was always seeking to facilitate reconciliation of persons
to God, to themselves, and to others. His deeds of mercy,
His message of hope, and His ethic of love opened paths
of redemption.

Christ's detractors scorned Him for refusing to exact
judgment and punishment from those whose lives were

marred by fear, error, defeat, and despair. Jesus said,
"Come to me, all who labor and are heavy laden, and I
will give you rest" (Matt. 11:28, RSV).

The Church must be that one place where together
we can learn how to discover God's will and grace in the
very difficult tasks and decisions that life thrusts on us.
Absolute perfection is not the goal. For most of us, that
possibility has long since disappeared in failed marriages,
business dealings gone bad, career paths that proved dis-
astrous, and friendships and family relationships that
have soured. In the community of grace, in the decisions
we make and the tasks we shoulder, redemption and the
sanctification of all life is the Christian goal. This is the vision that will guide our discussion of the Christian and
bioethics.

The Importance of the Family

For Christians, the family and the Church form the
primary setting for learning and living the Christian faith
(Eph. 5:21—6:4). Many Christians choose to remain single, an option blessed by the apostle Paul in 1 Cor. 7. No
one should disparage singleness as an appropriate form
for freedom, joy, and service as a Christian. Single persons, too, are parts of and contributors to families and vital members of the graced community. But for the Christian family there exists for parents a unique responsibility
and opportunity to teach and live the Christian story before their children.

Many of the questions raised by bioethics bear directly on the family. The responses we make should reflect our respect for the parental bond and its responsibilities. They should also evidence the importance we
attach to the marital covenant. The acids that can eat
away at families are many. The Church must show the
way to Christian alternatives.

2

CONVICTIONS THAT SHOULD GUIDE US

Some basic Christian convictions should shape our approach to bioethics. As we have said, Christians are persons whose character is formed by the story of God's self-disclosure and His creation of a people. Pivotal to the story is God's dialogue with His children and His incarnation in Jesus Christ. As the story shapes us, it gives birth to formative values or convictions by which we think, choose, and live. The apostle Paul said, "Have this mind among yourselves, which is yours in Christ Jesus" (Phil. 2:5, RSV). The norm for Christian life is not that we be governed by external constraints, but by internalized, owned convictions that express themselves in parallel virtues. The Christian ethic is first of all the internalized law of God, accomplished by the Spirit, that Christians experience as "the law of freedom" (see Gal. 5:1). Freedom in Christ is freedom *from* the Law as an external tyrant and freedom *for* the Law as the power of Christ at work in us, creating in us a love for the will and way of God. It is not license, but freedom to be conformed to the new and true humanity that Christ reveals. As stated earlier, Christians are to "put on the Lord Jesus Christ" (Rom. 13:14, RSV). This means living by grace alone in the power of the Holy Spirit.

We will now look at four pairs of primary Christian convictions as they relate to bioethics. The two parts in each pair exist in complementary tension.

Freedom and Stewardship[1]

Freedom

One of the most astonishing aspects of the story of God is that when creating man and woman, He did not create puppets. He desired that Adam and Eve and their offspring should reflect the divine freedom and love for each other that they saw Him extending to them. The covenant that God wanted to establish between himself and humanity, while not one between equals, had everything to do with dialogue and mutual love. It had nothing to do with mechanical, preprogrammed obedience. This was humanity's glory.

Amazingly, along with the freedom for dialogue and complementary love came the possibility of rejecting the freedom God offered and of choosing an alien "freedom" that places people against God. But in choosing to place ourselves against God, we got the opposite of what we expected. We harvested not freedom, but slavery to passions and idolatry to the gods of our own making. Humanity became its own strongest opponent. So, created in the image of God for freedom in love and community, whenever humans attempt to "find themselves" elsewhere, they in fact succeed only in losing their real identity (Rom. 1:16-32).

Christians are persons who have come to know that freedom in Christ is true freedom, not slavery. "I have called you friends," Jesus said in John 15:15. Christian freedom is freedom to act creatively and imaginatively in accordance with the character of God as the Holy Spirit forms God's character in us (Rom. 6:15-23). Strong, mature Christians bring glory to God.

The same principle applies to bioethics. We need not cringe in inactivity or cower in fear before developments in technology that show promise of improving the human condition. Nor should we be fearfully paralyzed in the presence of difficult decisions for which no sure path has yet been charted. We may be sure that in the arena of life, where difficult bioethical problems will have to be worked through, our Christian faith will equip and guide us.

Authentic discipleship is not a state of endless infancy and adolescence, but a robust freedom that comes through grace and that makes it possible to try, and even to fail, in the interest of love and human community.

Stewardship

Existing in creative tension with freedom is Christian stewardship. We will see how freedom includes stewardship, and stewardship includes freedom. Stewardship is one of the central symbols by which Christians are to understand their existence in the Church and in the world. According to the Christian vision of life in the world "human action takes place within a context in which humans are ultimately responsible to God as the sovereign Lord of life, Creator, Preserver, and Redeemer.[2]

The Bible refers to "steward" and "stewardship" more than 26 times. The terms refer to a servant, but not to an ordinary one. A steward is a superior servant, a sort of supervisor or foreman who must make decisions and give orders. A steward has latitude to act. In the Old Testament the one to whom the steward is responsible is usually a king or ruler. Failure to discharge one's responsibility could prompt the ruler to revoke the steward's position (see Gen. 43—44; Dan. 1:11, 16).[3] In the New Testament, the image of steward continues but achieves a higher level of meaning (Matt. 20:8; 21:33-41; Luke 8:3; John 2:8). Placed in a position of high trust and responsibility, the steward was supposed to exercise freedom, good judgment, and imagination in his care for the master's goods. The master expected a wise steward to enrich (*oikodomeo,* "build further") the value and quality of the estate. Hopefully, the steward would eventually hear, "Well done, thou good and faithful servant" (Matt. 25:21, KJV).

The way Jesus used the word "stewardship" is pivotal for understanding discipleship. In Luke 12:42-48, for example, Jesus identifies "stewardship" or "servant-hood" together with "watchfulness"—as requisite characteristics of His followers. Now Christ himself, rather than an earthly king, is the Master before whom and for whom stewardship is exercised. During the Lord's earthly absence, His disciples are responsible for their Master's "household" and for its occupants. Christ issues a stern warning to any steward who forgets his conferred status and begins to behave as though the household is his to do with as he pleases (Matt. 21:33-41; Luke 12:45-48).

In much of popular Christianity, stewardship has a very narrow meaning. Often it is limited to generating monetary support for the church. But stewardship includes far more. It involves recognizing that all the resources at our disposal—our bodies, education, the environment, and so forth—belong to God. He has entrusted them to us. As stewards, we must use all of those resources in creative ministry to God and in service to our neighbor (Rom. 6:15-23; 12:1-2). So stewardship is a link for understanding first of all who we *are* by God's grace and second what we're *to do* in response to God's grace. We can speak of "the gospel of Christian stewardship," for it is by the way we practice Christian stewardship that we proclaim and live the gospel of our Lord.

The steward must not only freely exercise his or her office *for* the Master but also act for the sake of his or her neighbor. Stewardship is freely exercised *before* the Master and *for* the many. The apostle Paul presents what is perhaps the most complete portrayal of Christian stewardship: "Let no one boast about human leaders. For all things are yours, whether Paul or Apollos or Cephas or the world or life or death or the present or the future—all belong to you, and you belong to Christ, and Christ belongs to God" (1 Cor. 3:21-23, NRSV).

The apostle Peter also contributes to the New Testament portrait of stewardship. He says that through their stewardship, Christians demonstrate that they attach ultimate significance to God alone, never to the goods, institutions, and securities of this world. The steward knows that the world gains its meaning only in relationship to God's gracious action *upon* it and the deeds He performs *in* it. The world belongs to God, not to itself. The way a Christian steward conducts himself or herself in the world ought to evidence allegiance to these convictions. Accordingly, Peter urged first-century Christians to keep sane and sober. They were to love one another, practice hospitality, and wisely employ the gifts they received from God. Each person should live as a good steward of God's grace, so that in all things God would be glorified (1 Pet. 4:10-11).

For Christians, Christ is the supreme model of stewardship. Our Lord claimed no independent importance for himself but took upon himself "the form of a slave, being born in human likeness" (Phil. 2:7, NRSV). So "because he is a just and faithful steward; because he desires nothing for himself; because he is obedient to the One he represents; Christ completes the office in a way that is redemptive for others."[4] The apostle Paul urges us to maintain a disposition toward life that matches the one Jesus demonstrated.

If the Christian understanding of stewardship is our way of life in the world, then it can guide us as we approach bioethics. First of all, as we live as stewards, our attitude toward technology and medical resources should differ from those who thoughtlessly treat it as a deity. Some people act as though they believe that if technology makes something possible, then it *ought* to be done. Christians think differently. No part of the world—technology included—should be permitted to just go its own way, as though it were of ultimate importance. We should exercise Christian stewardship over technology just as we do over any other part of God's creation. We should submit all of its manifestations to criticism by values that transcend it.

Second, by their conduct in the world, Christians

must demonstrate that the world belongs to God. God's
world should not be the victim of injustice and greedy exploitation. We should live in ways that demonstrate both
our confidence in the world's essential goodness and
God's ownership of it and its future in Christ. This implies
that our trust and hope are in the Lord, not in the temporary and shifting securities that some people try to
squeeze from earthly resources. For example, Christians
ought never to be found grasping for the last ounces of
physical life as though its death is the end of meaning.
Our physical life is not our own; it, too, is a part of the
steward's trust. Christian hope and joy mean in part that
we don't have to survive! Christians should learn both to
live and to *die* as stewards.

Third, stewardship also means that God has entrusted to us the task of cultivating His world. We are to enrich all that He has given to us. If properly governed, advances in health care and genetic research can
demonstrate our free, responsible, and creative stewardship. Christians should be at the forefront of scientific
creativity, demonstrating the full meaning of Christian
stewardship. We are God's creative stewards, not menial,
passive servants. Our creativity should demonstrate a
thirst for wholeness, justice, and mercy (Matt. 25:14-30).

The Sanctity and Relative Value of Human Life

The Sanctity of Human Life

Central to the Judeo-Christian tradition is the belief
that God is the principal Author of life. He is the Creator,
and all people everywhere stand in a unique and sacred
relation to Him. For Christians, "human" is first of all a
theological concept, not a sociological, psychological, or
economic one. We know what it means to be a person
first of all, with reference to our relationship to God. Personhood is a gift from God that should be cherished, nurtured, and preserved by all.

More specifically, our discussion of personhood begins with Christ, the head of the new and true humanity. To be sure, political, biological, sociological, psychological, and economic factors figure prominently in our understanding of personhood. But for Christians, such elements are of lesser significance and must always be referenced to Christ, the ultimate anthropological touchstone. All persons should be seen through the eyes of Christ, to whom the whole creation is the object of reconciliation (2 Cor. 5:14-21; Rom. 8:18-25).

Theologian Hans Walter Wolff says that in the Old Testament, person (or personhood) is characteristically understood in terms of a dialogue. Persons gain their significance in dialogue with God, a dialogue that He initiates. Humanity is called into question and searched out by God. When He asks Adam, "Where are you?" (Gen. 3:9), He is addressing all humanity. Humans are established not so much for what they are as for what they *are called to be* before God. Humanity is anything but the "measure of all things."[5]

What is uniquely human derives not only from being "of the dust of the earth" but also from a unique relationship to God, who breathes into humanity's nostrils the breath of life. All attempts to know what personhood is by looking primarily to the world alone will in the end lead to humanity becoming the most alien creature of all.[6]

Human life is sacred, but it does not have absolute value. Sometimes Christians mistakenly say that human life has *intrinsic* value. "Intrinsic" means having value *in and of itself,* without reference to any other thing or person beyond itself. This may be a correct way to speak of humans if one is a secular humanist who insists on human autonomy and believes that people establish their value simply by being human. But Christians reject this notion. We believe in the "bestowed" value of persons, not in their intrinsic value. Persons have *inviolable* value not because of what they can establish or defend as their own, but because of the value God assigns to them as His handiwork. This estimate of human value, we Christians believe, assigns a higher dignity and value to persons than does the secular notion of intrinsic value.

For Christians, a person is significant not because of the political, economic, or social turf he or she can command. Neither is a person significant only from contributing to a nation's net monetary worth or if he or she matches some artificial "genetic norm." Rather, a person has inviolable value *simply because God values him or her.* And because He does, so ought we. The apostle Paul said that Christians ought not to evaluate others based on what the world thinks of them (2 Cor. 5:16). The highest expression of God's bestowal of value upon all persons, and the standard by which we are to appraise others, is that He gave His only begotten Son to restore all persons—without reference to social status—to divine fellowship.

Therefore, the life of one person must never be treated simply as a means for satisfying the selfish desires of another. To do so violates the sanctity of life. For Christians, no monetary, institutional, or national interests should be permitted to violate this principle. People are objects of divine communion, not exploitation.

Although the Christian ethic endorses the principle of the sanctity of life without qualification, its consistent application is not so easily achieved. For instance, should Christians participate in war and thereby kill other persons? Many believe that all war is a glaring violation of the sanctity of life. Others are confident that refusing to defend one's country and its citizens tramples the sanctity of life. Christians equally committed to the sanctity of life will have a difficult time reaching agreement regarding war. Failure to respect either Christian conviction can lead to conflict among well-meaning persons. We should admit this up front.

The Scriptures, Christian tradition, and experience all

tell us that we live in a fallen world. At times we are caught in tragedies, some of which are not of our making. Values will inevitably sometimes conflict. For example, two people, both of whom God values, may be in need of a kidney transplant when only one is available. Sanctity of life alone provides an inadequate guide for deciding between the two persons.

The Relative Value of Human Life

While Christians believe in the inviolable value of life as established by God, they also believe that one's security and significance do not rest upon physical or mental well-being. Christian hope doesn't depend on feeding tubes, ventilators, and laser surgery. A Christian's hope and identity as a person rests solidly on the reality that nothing can separate him or her from the love of God as manifest in Christ (Rom. 8:31-39). While physical life can have rich significance, and while it can be a means through which God is worshiped (12:1-2), it nevertheless has relative, not absolute, value. Simply, Christians can die without their meaning being destroyed. While death can certainly temporarily separate Christians from much that they love, it cannot separate them from meaning. And it will not finally separate them even from their transformed bodies (1 Cor. 15:35-58). For Christians, "life" means primarily not physical life, but eternal life— that is, life in Christ and in His kingdom. So physical life is of value, but only relatively so. Its value is indexed to something higher than itself.

From the second pair of convictions, Christians can anticipate implications for bioethics. We know that our value before God does not depend on mutable and transitory circumstances. Therefore, we don't have to cling to physical life as though it were the last light in the house. We need not in panic try to wring the last drop of physical life from a diseased and tortured body. When appropriate, Christians can confidently release their borrowed breath back into the hands of their God, knowing that He will never leave them nor forsake them. Christians who understand their faith ought to die different from those "who have no hope" (1 Thess. 4:13; see also 1 Cor. 15:12-28).

The sanctity and relative value of human life guard against two dangers we face in bioethics. The first is to devalue persons because society judges them undesirable or because they can't justify their value through economic or social status. The second danger is to greedily consume limited therapeutic resources when they could have a much greater salutary impact somewhere else. Swiss theologian Karl Barth warned Christians against worshiping health. But he also urged them to "improve, raise and perhaps radically transform the general living conditions of all men." Perhaps this will even require "a new and quite different order of society, guaranteeing better living conditions for all." [7]

Individuality and Social Solidarity

In the third pair of pivotal Christian convictions, we learn that in the Christian faith the *individual* person is important, but individuality is always understood relationally. United States civil rights leader Martin Luther King Jr. wrote in his "Letter from a Birmingham Jail" (April 16, 1963), "I am cognizant of the interrelatedness of all communities and states. . . . Injustice anywhere is a threat to justice everywhere. We are caught in an inescapable network of mutuality, tied in a single garment of destiny. Whatever affects one directly, affects all indirectly." [8]

Theologian Hans Walter Wolff says that in the life of ancient Israel the individual was always firmly integrated into the bonds of his or her family and thus of his or her people. "Wherever [the individual] is set apart or isolated, something unusual, if not something threatening" is occurring. [9]

Christian ethicist Paul Ramsey in his covenant-centered Christian ethic developed this third pair of convictions. According to Ramsey, God has made a covenant with people who therefore have an obligation to be faithful to that covenant by repeating it in all their relationships with others. Faithfulness to the covenant requires parallel fidelity between persons.[10] Throughout, the biblical record presents a picture of human life as essentially *personal* and as essentially *relational.* Both are required.

A Christian understanding of individuality is distinctly different from the narcissistic (excessive and destructive self-love) perception of individuality so evident in our culture. Most advertising, the names of many magazines, and the entertainment media reflect our culture's obsession with the individual.

By contrast, in both the Old and New Testaments, the individual is a person only in relationship to others. Though individuality is affirmed (for example, think of how often the apostle Paul refers to himself), it is never complete apart from community, apart from the neighbor.

The Christian understanding places the individual in essential social solidarity with his or her neighbor. This conviction flatly opposes all isolationist perceptions of personhood. The Christian conviction fosters responsibility. It raises a strong counter voice against the unchecked egoism that often creeps into the development and use of biotechnology. A Christian understanding of personhood should lead Christians to temper individual interests with global and neighborly concerns. For example, Christians should raise a united voice against the inequitable distribution of medical resources in the world. They should work to correct the inequality of access to health care between first world and developing countries, as well as within wealthy nations.

David Neff in *Christianity Today* wrote that when Christians speak regarding bioethics, they should be alert to the special needs of those who cannot care or speak for themselves. These include the unborn, the catastrophically ill, and the aged and infirm. "Approaches to bioethics that do not put first the needs of the weak and defenseless must be resisted" as contrary to Christian norms, he says.[11]

A Christian Appraisal of Technology

The fourth Christian conviction that guides our discussion of bioethics arises from what we believe about God's relationship to the world, and hence to technology.[12] Christians believe that like any other part of creation, technology has an important role to play in God's design for creation. In an important sense, we find a measure of personal fulfillment through the tools we produce and use. Anyone who has ever stood back and admired a job well done will understand this.

The word "technology" comes from two Greek words. The first, *techne,* means "art, trade, or craft." The second, *logos,* means "word or speech." We use reason to make things considered useful. Daniel Bell of Harvard University has identified six essential dimensions of technology: function, energy, fabrication, communication, control, and regulated decision making.[13]

Christians are aware that technology can be used for either good or destructive ends. We have witnessed many abuses of technology and the tragedies that can result. Our doctrine of original sin predisposes us to be always alert to the likelihood that technology will be pressed into evil's service. On March 10, 2000, the Federal Bureau of Investigation in Kansas City began to investigate a local pathologist suspected of profiteering from the sale of tissues from fetuses at a clinic where abortions are performed. Members of a congressional subcommittee requested the probe. Federal law requires that fees associated with obtaining fetal tissue for research be no more than the cost of fetal-tissue removal and transportation. The pathologist told an undercover ABC News reporter that fetal organs such as livers, hearts, and brains are in high demand and that researchers "will pay whatever you ask." The pathologist showed the reporter a price list for the organs. "There is clearly a for-profit, market-driven sale of body parts," said Steve Schmidt, spokesman for the House Commerce Committee."[14]

Such abuses are inevitable. But instead of treating technology and the risks that come with it as inherently evil, Christians recognize that the imagination and intelligence that produce technology are gifts from God. Human creativity reflects the divine creativity that brought the world into existence and that even now sustains it. If human engineers amaze us, what are we to think of the Master Engineer, who takes four chemical ingredients and constructs the entire genetic code? Joyce Tombran-Tink, a Christian scientist engaged in cancer research, says, "Sometimes in my lab as I trace God's creativity in the genetic code, I just cry in astonishment."

Many Christian thinkers have come to understand that modern science and technology have their roots in the Hebraic view of the cosmos. In the Hebraic understanding of God's relationship to the cosmos, the world is divested of divinity. It does not claim to be God. The planets, the seasons, the fertility of the earth, as well as human fertility, are in no way divine. God created them. He stands above all of them as their Creator and Sustainer. In the best sense of the word, the world is secular, not sacred (divine). Only in God's presence does the world receive its meaning.

This posture gives humanity new freedom. Instead of fearing the world or being its servant, we are God-appointed stewards over it. A world that is secular is one that we can investigate and develop. Jack W. Moore puts it this way, "Humans can be co-workers with God's creative activity in maintaining and improving the patterns and processes of nature." This stewardship he says, is both our right and responsibility. God has designed the natural order and we must respect that order if we are to preserve the structures of our humanity.[15]

In the Hebraic-Christian vision of God and the world, men and women never stand alone before creation to do with it as they please. When viewed correctly, the world is not the plaything of our arrogance and lust. The marvelous beauty and possibilities wrapped up in the world exist not primarily in relationship to persons, but to God. "The earth is the LORD'S, and the fulness thereof" (Ps. 24:1, KJV).

The most important point to observe in the relationship between the two is that wisdom must always govern, not prohibit, technology. "Knowing why" must monitor "knowing how." But the two should be mutually complementary, each enriching the other. For example, think of how John Gutenberg's printing press (technology) has enriched the pursuit of wisdom. The same can be said of the Internet.

A Christian approach encourages a complementary development of both wisdom and technology. We believe that both are parts of what it means to reflect God in the world. But we insist that wisdom must always govern technology. And we believe that worship of God is the beginning of wisdom. We must always be mindful of our divine vocation in the world. We are stewards of know-how, not its masters. But secular humanists do not view humanity's role in the world as a divine vocation. Consequently, they do not appraise technology with reference to God as the chief end of all human endeavors.

When it comes to how we regard technology, Christians should be guardedly optimistic. But this is true only as we submit technology to regulation by transcendent values and to wide thinking that includes human and cosmic well-being. Freeman Dyson of Princeton University, a mathematician and physicist who in 1948 tied together contrasting theories of quantum electrodynamics, pointedly states the task before us: "To lift up poor countries, and poor people in rich countries . . . technology is not enough. Technology must be guided and driven by ethics if it is to do more than provide toys for the rich."[16]

PART 2

Issues of Life and Death

Medical technology has increasingly permitted us to control the conditions under which persons are born, live, and die. Most of us will at some time benefit directly from these advances. But we will also have to deal with some difficult questions that technological advances generate.

Without warning, families are often called upon to make decisions regarding access to medical technology. In this section we are going to examine some of the bio-medical options that inevitably present moral challenges.

3

ABORTION

Rachael Blanding is a 24-year-old single parent who has a two-year-old son. Two months ago, because of Christian love shown to her by a couple in your Sunday School class, Rachael has taken steps toward becoming a Christian. Now she is attending your Sunday School class.

Rachael has had a rough life. Married first at 17, she has since divorced twice. She is currently three months pregnant.

Rachael has known for four years that she has a valvular heart disease. Last night she was admitted to the hospital with acute congestive heart failure. Intensive care has stabilized her life, but the use of a respirator and cardiopulmonary assistance will be required to maintain her life over the next six days.

Given her precarious position, Rachael is being advised to terminate the pregnancy (dilation and extraction) as the safest course of action.

What should she do?

The Debate over Abortion

Few subjects provoke stronger feelings or generate a wider range of opinions than does induced abortion, here defined as the intentional use of artificial means to terminate a pregnancy. Abortion is not to be confused with a miscarriage, which is a natural abortion.[1] The debate over abortion has sharply divided the people of the United States. Former United States Surgeon General C. Everett Koop said of the controversy, "Nothing like it has separated our society since the days of slavery."

The debate over abortion is between those who support "the right to an abortion" and those who believe that induced abortion, except perhaps in rare permissible instances, means killing a defenseless person. Those of the "pro-choice" persuasion insist that fundamental to a woman's dignity is the "right" to choose an abortion. If society were to deny to women the "right" to seek an abortion when they think they should, then their own personhood would have been seriously infringed upon.[2] On the other hand, those who oppose "induced abortion on request" believe that abortion shows gross moral irresponsibility because it violates the "rights" of the fetus, the "right to life." Arguments in support of each position have been offered without end.

Currently the debate in the United States seems to be at an impasse. This should not be surprising. The two positions rest on mutually exclusive premises. Decades more of debate based on the current polarized positions will likely not convince either side.

The first position, that of the pro-choice camp, sets out from the belief that a woman should have control over her own body, her own reproductive functions. This includes deciding whether or not a fetus should be brought to term. The fetus has no independent moral status—actually, it has no moral status at all in this view. Consequently, terminating it by abortion is not seen as a moral wrong. Instead, "wrong" applies when the "legitimate rights" of the woman are subordinated to the "alleged rights" of the fetus. The fetus will gain "moral status" when separated by birth from the mother. For supporters of pro-choice, this position seems abundantly obvious.

Pro-choice arguments additionally rely on the elevation of the "private" morality of women over the "public" morality of men. In this spirit, pro-choice supporters define abortion as an intensely personal experience that no one (particularly no male) can judge. Prohibition against abortion is largely an artificial ethic imposed on women by men who have traditionally denied "personhood" for women and who have never experienced the oppression that results when males are the principal shapers of "right" and "wrong" in a society, they say. The most radical form of this position claims total reproductive autonomy, free of any suggestion of obligation or external (societal) constraint.

The second position, that of the pro-life camp, rests upon the conviction that the fetus does have a recognizable moral status that must be respected. The fetus is a person under development, as all of us are, they say. The notion that the woman should control the fate of the fetus without there being any legitimately recognizable moral claims the fetus can make is thought to be absurd. For supporters of the "pro-life" position, the fetus has "rights" to life as any other person, not because a mother "benevolently" grants the fetus permission to live. The woman cannot successfully claim personhood for herself and at the same time deny the same quality to the fetus she carries. For supporters of pro-life, this position seems abundantly obvious.

There is disagreement among pro-life supporters regarding the point in a pregnancy when human life begins. There is also disagreement regarding the conditions, if any, under which an abortion is morally defensible.

On one end of the spectrum are some who think that since the fetus had absolutely no say in coming into existence, if a choice must be made between the life of the fetus and the life of the mother, the fetus should receive primary consideration. At the other end are what we might call the "contextualists," who believe that the fetus has moral significance that must be respected. But they identify a range of circumstances or contexts in which an abortion, even though tragic, would be morally justifiable. Even among contextualists there is disagreement. Some would permit an abortion only if the mother's life is clearly in danger, others in the event of a pregnancy caused by incest or rape or if the mother's life is at serious risk. For others the range of factors might include severe physical but non-life-threatening illness by the mother or perhaps domestic trauma generated by the pregnancy. Still others would allow factors such as discernible genetic birth defects (such Down syndrome or anencephaly) as a defensible reason for abortion.

Contextualists maintain that a person may, under limited conditions, abort a fetus and that such a choice can be judged morally responsible. For the contextualist, the "quality of life" as well as the "sanctity of fetal life" are important factors when considering abortion as an alternative to a full-term pregnancy. The contextualist tries to find a balance between these two values. He or she insists that the fetus ought to be protected against unrestricted freedom to abort. Contextualists are often at odds with "pro-life" supporters on the other end of the spectrum.

No simple profile of pro-life supporters can accurately be drawn. Take Kellyanne Fitzpatrick, for instance. She is resolutely a young, conservative woman who supports women's rights. For her, abortion is not a women's issue. Speaking for others who share her position, she says the central issue in the abortion controversy is not about a woman's right to control her own body, but rather the reality of a visibly moving fetus that is fully human. Speaking to those who support abortion on the basis of women's rights, Fitzpatrick says, "You can't appeal to us through our wombs. We're pro-life. The fetus beat us. We grew up with sonograms. We know life when we see it."[3]

In the debate over abortion, suspicions fly regarding the motives and moral honesty of both sides. Neither position believes that the other is being morally responsible. Those who support the right to abortion think that their opponents are generally ignorant of the urgent and morally defensible reasons for which women around the world seek abortions. Those who oppose "abortion on demand" are just as certain that their opponents are insensitive to the value of the life in the woman's womb.

Roe v. Wade:
The Current United States Legal Standard

The landmark Supreme Court decision on the legality of abortion in the United States occurred in 1973. By a seven-to-two majority, the court ruled that women have a constitutional right to an abortion for at least the first six months of pregnancy. After that, the state can establish limitations. The court held that "the right of personal privacy includes the abortion decision" (*Roe v. Wade*, 410 U.S. 113, 93 S. Ct. 705 [1972]). The justices who represented the majority position said that based on the legal, moral, and medical arguments, it was impossible for the court to reach a generally supportable conclusion as to when human life begins.

Prior to *Roe v. Wade*, abortion laws in the United States constituted something of a legal jungle, a situation that had grown in magnitude since abortion was first ruled illegal in the United States. Contrary to popular opinion, the legal strictures against abortion were of comparatively recent origin. Until the early 19th century, in common law in England and the United States, abortion "before quickening" was not illegal at all. It became so only in the early 1800s.

After *Roe v. Wade*, the number of abortions performed annually in the United States rose fairly regularly until 1990, when the number reached 1,608,600. Then, in 1991, the number began to drop, with 1,556,500 performed that year. In 1997 the estimated number was 1,365,730. The total number of abortions in the United States since 1973 stands at approximately 38,010,378 (there is a rate of 3 percent possibly underreported).

On January 6, 2000, the Centers for Disease Control and Prevention in Atlanta reported that the number of legal abortions in the United States fell in 1997 to the lowest level in two decades: 1,184,758, or 3 percent less than the 1,221,585 abortions in 1996. Possible reasons given for the decline were (1) reduced access to abortion services, (2) an increased willingness to use contraception, and (3) possible changing attitudes regarding the moral implications of abortion.[5]

Although subsequent court decisions qualified *Roe v. Wade* in some ways, the 1973 decision remained the uniform law of the land until in July 1989. In that year a bitterly divided Supreme Court voted seven to two to give the states greater control over the conditions under which abortions are permissible.

Why Women Choose Abortion

The reasons women give for choosing an abortion are many: They have had all the children they want. They want to delay their next birth. They are too young or too poor to raise a child. They are estranged from or on uneasy terms with their sexual partner. They do not want a child while they are in school or working outside the home.[6]

About 26 million women have legal abortions each year, and an additional 20 million have abortions in countries where abortion is restricted or prohibited by law. In much of the world, liberalization of abortion laws occurred rapidly between 1950 and 1985. By early 1986, 36 countries had liberal abortion laws, permitting women to obtain the procedure for social or medical reasons, or some other reason.[7]

The "Morning After Pill": RU-486

An important element has been added to the controversy, one that significantly altered the field of debate. In the 1980s a French drug maker introduced a product that could reliably induce an early abortion. The pills had to be taken three at a time, to be followed a few days later with an additional drug. Mifepristone, or RU-486, must be administered by a physician trained in the two-step, two-drug process. It causes a controlled miscarriage weeks before most doctors would attempt a surgical abortion.[8] The drug caught on quickly in France, Sweden, the United Kingdom, and China. In the United States it remained off the market. At first this was because of political forces and later because of business blunders by United States developers.

Then, after intense public debate, on September 18, 1997, the Federal Drug Administration (FDA) conditionally approved mifepristone for use in the United States. "Conditional" meant that the FDA awaited more information from clinical trials about the drug's manufacture and labeling. Advocates for legally introducing RU-486 into the United States held that the availability of mifepristone would help ensure women's privacy. It would also enhance their ability to make reproductive health decisions free of pro-life violence, blockades, and harassment.[9]

In spite of conditional FDA approval of RU-486, public debate continued. On June 24, 1998, the House of Representatives passed an amendment that would prevent the FDA from using government funds to test or approve the use of drugs that induce abortion. The bill, which provided that no funds "may be used by the FDA for the testing, development, or approval (including approval of production, manufacturing, or distribution) of any drug for the chemical inducement of abortion," passed on a 223-202 vote. At the beginning of 2000, the future of the bill was uncertain. To become law, a similar bill would have to be passed by the Senate and signed by the president (or a presidential veto would have to be overridden). Opponents of the bill insisted that a ban on FDA funding would impose an undue burden on women seeking an early, medical abortion.

The Current Debate over Partial-Birth Abortion

One form of abortion currently being heatedly debated in state legislatures, in the press, and among the United States citizenry is partial-birth abortion. Though rarely used, it is highly controversial. President Bill Clinton had by late 1999 twice vetoed proposed federal laws banning partial birth abortions. In October 1999 the United States Senate again passed the legislation. But it fell two votes short of the number needed to override a presidential veto. As an example of legislative action in the state legislatures, in September 1999 the Missouri General Assembly overrode Gov. Mel Carnahan's veto of legislation banning partial-birth abortion. As of November 1999 as many as 30 states had laws regulating this procedure.

Partial-birth abortions are unlike other abortions, in which the fetus is destroyed within the womb. Partial-birth abortion kills an already partially delivered fetus. Part of the procedure involves breaking the mother's bag of water. Then, using forceps, the doctor turns the fetus around in the womb to a position in which the feet will exit first. The fetus is then pulled out, except for the head. After the partial delivery, scissors are forced into the base of the skull, and suction is used to remove the brains. Delivery of the now-dead fetus is then completed.[10]

What Our Language and Actions Say About Abortion

Many people think that in spite of the arguments offered in support of abortion rights, the language we use in our society when speaking of the fetus has revealed how people really assess its status. On the one hand, if the pregnancy is wanted, we consistently speak of the fetus as a "baby." Advertisers, family members, and friends of the expectant parents consistently use the language associated with personhood. But if the pregnancy is not desired, then the language used to describe the fetus changes, being carefully sanitized as referring to something whose future is completely at the discretion of the pregnant woman.

Many people wonder how the moral status of the fetus can be switched simply by a change in language. How, they ask, can simply desiring or not desiring the full-term birth of the fetus change its status? Is personhood a quality that we can simply assign or withhold at will?

America's contradiction in language is surpassed only by its contradictory actions. Chief Court Justice Sandra Day O'Connor observed that *"Roe v. Wade* is on a collision course with itself." She was referring to medical advances since 1973 that make it easier both to destroy potential life and to preserve it. Her meaning is vividly illustrated by those rare but disturbing cases in which a second- or third-trimester abortion yields a living infant. The infant must either be killed, which would be judged murder, or rushed to another part of the hospital for the latest in expensive neonatal care.[11]

If the infant is placed in neonatal care, we will bend heaven and earth to save it. But in other circumstances, killing the same infant by partial-birth abortion, had the mother and physician chosen to do so, would have been judged morally permissible by many.

A mother who intentionally kills a premature infant after giving birth will receive both legal and social condemnation. But if she were to destroy the same "premie" through partial-birth abortion, many persons would protect her "rights."

How long, opponents of abortion on demand ask, can we live with such moral and legal contradictions?

What the Bible Has to Say About Abortion

Abortion is of grave concern to Christians on both sides of the debate. It is proper that they would look to the Scriptures for guidance. When the Scriptures do provide clear guidance, they should be employed. But we must be wary of trying to support any position on a faulty interpretation. Respected New Testament scholar Richard B. Hays says, "The Bible contains no texts about abortion," even though "a few texts poetically declare God's providential care for all of life, even before birth or conception."[12] Our respect for the Bible should keep us from forcing the Bible to say either more or less than it says clearly.

Numerous scriptural passages are often cited for supporting either side of the abortion argument, but upon careful examination, they do not clearly support an absolutist position, either pro-life or pro-choice. When absolutist conclusions are drawn, they rely on questionable deductions that are not necessitated by the scripture in question. The scriptures commonly appealed to are Exod. 21:22-25; Job 3:3; 10:8-9; Pss. 51:5; 139:13-15; Isa. 49:1, 5; Luke 1:41 ff.; Gal. 1:15; Heb. 7:9-10. All of these passages receive differing interpretations from equally faithful and competent interpreters of the Bible.

Of the scriptures noted above, the passage that seems to speak most directly to the subject of abortion is Exod. 21:22-25. Both pro-life and pro-choice supporters believe that these verses support their respective positions: "If men who are fighting hit a pregnant woman and she gives birth prematurely but there is no serious injury, the offender must be fined whatever the woman's husband demands and the court allows. But if there is serious injury, you are to talk life for life, eye for eye, tooth for tooth, hand for hand, foot for foot, burn for burn, wound for wound, bruise for bruise."

Upon turning to the commentaries, one discovers extensive disagreement among the scholars regarding the meaning of these verses. The disagreement makes it impossible to draw rigid conclusions regarding which side of the current abortion controversy the verses support or whether they even address the subject at all. Some interpretations seem to support one position, others an opposite position, while still others support neither.

The most preferable way to assess Exod. 21:22-25 is

to admit the ambiguity of the text. The verses simply do not make clear whether the phrase "gives birth prematurely" should be taken to mean a miscarriage or a premature birth in which the child continues to live. Neither is it clear whether the phrase "serious injury" refers to the mother or to the fetus.

There are no explicit references to abortion in the New Testament. It is possible that the association of the use of drugs *(pharmakeia)* with abortion in pagan and later Christian writings indicates a reference to abortion in such texts as Gal. 5:20 and Rev. 9:21; 18:23; 21:8; and 22:15. In some instances *pharmakeia* was used to refer to poisons and mind-disturbing drugs. In one instance it refers specifically to the use of one type of evil drug, the abortifacient. So the word can, but need not, mean the use of drugs or evil or magical drugs or a specific evil drug such as a poison or an abortifacient.[13]

Only once does the term *ektroma* (abortion, aborted, or untimely birth) appear in the Bible (1 Cor. 15:8). In this instance Paul uses the word metaphorically to refer to his own apostleship. It has nothing to do with aborting a human fetus.

Though we must be cautious when examining the scriptures on this issue, there is much in the Bible that does bear on the rightness or wrongness of abortion. The Bible clearly teaches that God is the Creator of men and women and the Author of human life (Gen. 1:26-27; 2:7; Ps. 8). It teaches that He is active in the conception and birth of a human life (Gen. 20:18; 30:2; Ruth 4:13; Luke 1:22-24, 36-37) and that He is constant in His care for life even before birth (Job 31:15; Ps. 22:9; Isa. 44:2, 24; 49:1, 5, 15; Jer. 1:5; Luke 1:23-25, 36-45). Because humanity is the bearer of God's image, human life comes under the protection of the divine commandment against killing another human being (Gen. 9:6; Exod. 20:13; 21:12, 14; Matt. 5:21). Sexual relationships are assigned serious value (1 Cor. 6:16), even a sanctified value (7:1 ff.; 1 Thess.

4:3-6), which, in turn, involves the rejection of illegitimate sexual relationships (Matt. 5:32 ff.; Mark 10:11, 19 ff.; 1 Cor. 6:9 ff.). Nowhere does Scripture intimate that human life can be arbitrarily destroyed without violating God's covenant with us (Exod. 21:12-16; Rom. 13:4).

Toward a Christian Assessment of Abortion

Attempts to answer the question of whether abortion is right or wrong are made by (1) fixing a particular point at which a fetus becomes a person and (2) arguing for the "rights" of the fetus have their value. But Christians make a mistake when they use these arguments as their primary strategy for dealing with abortion. The first approach is too clinical, and the second is too naturalistic. The major importance of the Bible in this matter does not lie in our being able to find specific instances in which abortion is condemned (or approved) or the status of the fetus specified. The effort to find proof texts as though searching for legal decrees is a weak approach for Christians.

New Testament scholar Richard B. Hays, who recognizes that the Bible does not explicitly treat the topic of abortion, says that we must place the topic in "the broader framework of the New Testament's *symbolic world* and then reflect analogically about the way the New Testament might provide implicit" guidance. Hays draws the following conclusions:

According to the New Testament, God is the author of life. All life comes into being through the creative agency of Christ, the Gospel of John declares. True to the New Testament, wherever new life begins to develop in any pregnancy, the creative power of God is at work, and Jesus Christ, who was the original agent of creation, has already died for the redemption of the incipient life *in utero*. . . . We are privileged to participate in the creative work of God through begetting and bearing and birthing children, but there can

be no new life without the generative power of God.
We scatter seed, and it sprouts and grows without our
knowing how. As God's creatures, we are stewards
who bear life in trust. To terminate a pregnancy is not
only to commit an act of violence, but also to assume
responsibility for destroying a work of God, "from
whom are all things and for whom we exist" (1 Cor.
8:6). . . . Whether we accord "personhood" to the unborn child or not, he or she is a manifestation of new
life that has come forth from God.[14]

When speaking of the meaning of life as viewed
within the fellowship of the Holy Spirit (the Church), we
ought not to speak of individual "rights." The New Testament does not regard the issue of rights as a primary
Christian interest. As a matter of fact, preoccupation with
personal rights and freedoms by members of the Corinthi-
an church almost fragmented that community beyond repair. In 1 Corinthians, Paul deals forcefully with Corinthi-
an Christians whose discipleship was still oriented
toward themselves rather than toward the life of the community. Life in the Kingdom, by Paul's view of the matter,
ought to be marked primarily by concern for one's neighbor and for creating a community, a *koinonia*, that over-
comes the tyranny and isolation of selfishness and frag-
mentation. The Christological hymn of Phil. 2 is marked
by the fact that the Son of God did not "demand his
rights." And we are to have this mind in ourselves.

The language of rights we hear in today's world is
principally oriented toward the self. But the language of
the New Testament is about the grace of our Lord Jesus
Christ, about covenant, and about a redemptive event
through which a merciful God freely includes aliens and
former enemies in His kingdom. As Christians, we receive God's favor *not by right,* but by grace alone. Grace
and covenant constitute the primary reality of Christian
existence, and this is the foundation and substance of our
lives.

We receive our value from God. *For Christians, this should qualify all other standards and should fix the way we view others, especially the defenseless.* People can never be ignored, victimized, or eliminated simply because they are powerless by this world's standards. To do so opposes the gospel of Jesus Christ. First-century Christians seemed radical in the way they respected the personhood of slaves, women, and children. When the Early Church opposed infanticide, it did so out of regard for infants as objects of God's care even though they didn't have the social or political leverage to defend themselves.

Simply, Christians are to receive the other person as a trust and to see themselves as stewards of this trust. Jesus said that we meet and minister to *Him in* our neighbor. He even specified the *vulnerable* neighbor (Matt. 25:31-46). The value of oneself and of the other is, in fact, *a conferred value.* A person has value because of a relationship with God as Creator and not because of intrinsic value (the value something has in and of itself without relying on or being related to anything else). Were a person to have intrinsic value, there would no longer be any reason to base one's value in God.

The developing fetus in the womb *ought to be protected,* not on the grounds that it can claim legal or physiological humanity, but because of the way God's grace and mercy toward the world teaches us to treat those who are unable to speak for or defend themselves. Our highest example is the way God deals with us in Jesus Christ.

In summary, for Christians, the status of the developing child in the womb ought not to be primarily determined legally but *graciously.* Because the value of the developing child is conferred by God, he or she ought to be received into covenantal relationship—brought under the protection of the covenant of God's grace—in utero. Our attitude toward the developing child in the womb ought to demonstrate the way God's grace secures the insecure, protects the defenseless, and expands the boundaries of community and covenant.

The decision to abort a fetus should never be decided on the basis of convenience, selfishness, or even its legal status. Christians have long recognized that civil law may be inferior to the Christian standard. In light of our observations about the value of personhood and the extent of the Christian covenant, we conclude that the fetus demands our respect. Casual violation of its conferred value is a flagrant violation of the gospel. The philosophy that views the fetus as having no moral or religious significance is in conflict with the gospel of Christ.

Richard B. Hays concludes that "there might be circumstances in which we would deem the termination [of the unborn child] warranted, but the burden of proof lies heavily upon any decision to undertake such extreme action." The overall vision of the Bible would lead us to believe that the "normal response to pregnancy, within the Bible's symbolic world, is one of rejoicing for God's gift—even when that gift comes unexpectedly."[15]

No one can or should establish a list of circumstances under which an induced abortion could be justified. Such a code could never adequately explain all the factors that might make an abortion necessary as a part of a broader redemptive and healing effort. There may be instances in which abortion is a selfless act not intended to violate the value God places upon the fetus. There may even be times in which abortion protects the dignity of the fetus. Amid much heartache, parents may choose to abort a genetically deformed fetus, believing that their action shows greater respect for their child than to bring it to birth and then to a grotesque living death. Other Christians might encounter similar circumstances and conclude that it is *wrong* to abort.

One of the most imaginative efforts in the United States to provide a positive alternative to abortion for women faced with a crisis pregnancy is the Nurturing

Network of Boise, Idaho. Founded by Mary Cunningham
Agee in 1985, it is an international charitable organization in which, setting politics and rhetoric aside, volunteer members provide practical, life-saving services to
women facing the crisis of an unplanned pregnancy. Almost 12,500 mothers and children have been served
through the Nurturing Network, which seeks to insure
that every woman learns that the resources she needs to
continue her pregnancy are available.[16] The Nurturing
Network represents many similar positive alternatives to
abortion.

4

THE RIGHT TO DIE
AND EUTHANASIA

Ron and Cindy

Ron

Ron is 53 years old. He has been a member of the church since childhood and has been the choir director for 11 years. His positive attitude toward life attracts others. Ron is single and has one sister and two nieces. Both of his parents are deceased. Six months ago, Ron was diagnosed with acute myelogenous leukemia (a disease in which too many white blood cells are made in the bone marrow).

He has watched friends go through chemotherapy only to succumb eventually to a painful death. Years ago Ron made up his mind that if ever he were to contract any form of cancer as serious as the one he now has, he would reject what he calls "the modern indecencies" of a painful and certain death. True to his plans, he now refuses chemotherapy.

Ron is an educated and articulate person. He is quite aware that he will certainly die without treatment. As might be expected, he is upset by his diagnosis. But he is not depressed. His sister, brother-in-law, and close friends have urged him to accept treatment. They do not want him to die. Most, however, have honored his refusal.

But some members of the church have condemned Ron for showing what they call a lack of faith in God's power to heal. Some have even gone so far as to question whether Ron is really a Christian.

Ron understands that his death will likely be painful and may be prolonged. Unbeknownst to his family and friends, Ron has decided that at an appropriate point in the dying process, he will request a supply of barbiturates for ending his life.

Cindy

Cindy is a 45-year-old woman with two teenage children. Her husband has never been very supportive of her, and she has effectively raised the children by herself. For years she has struggled in her Christian faith. But she has tried to attend church regularly and to keep her children active in the children's and youth programs. Life for the three of them has been difficult.

Fourteen days ago Cindy's children brought her to the hospital emergency room. She was complaining of severe "migraine" headaches and had gained no relief from the medicine she normally used. While sitting in the waiting room, Cindy experienced a sharp pain in her left temple. She slid out of her chair, unconscious.

The triage nurse ran to help. Personnel quickly inserted a tube directly into her trachea to restore breathing and placed her on a ventilator, because her breathing efforts were labored and shallow. Cindy was whisked away to have a CAT (computerized axial tomography) scan. The test showed that she had a ruptured aneurysm in her left temporal lobe. She was immediately taken for brain surgery to have the aneurysm "clipped."

Today Cindy is still unconscious and on the ventilator in the intensive care unit. EEG's (electroencephalography) of the brain function show abnormal waveforms indicative of seizure activity. Cindy has not awakened from her surgery. Occasionally her eyelids flicker. She still has a gag reflex. Spontaneous movement is noted in her left arm and leg. But she is paralyzed on her right side. She turns her head to the left and ignores the right side of her body completely. The doctors have told her husband, children, and pastor that she has lost vision in her right eye. The doctors want to place a tracheotomy in her neck for an airway. The endotracheal tube has rubbed her lips and tongue raw. It is swollen and protruding.

Bill, Cindy's husband, cannot see any real future for his wife. The doctor's prognosis is that if she does make it off the ventilator, she will need constant care, including a feeding tube and urinary tube. Bill kisses his wife's shaved head—and then requests that the ventilator be removed.

In the 20th century we have witnessed astonishing advances in the ability of medical science to sustain human life. New drugs, artificially supplied nutrition, respirators, cardiovascular resuscitators, renal dialysis machines, and hydration are advances that constitute a mixed blessing.

Technology has dramatically increased the rate of recovery for victims of diseases and illnesses that a few years ago were almost always fatal. Millions of people today have an opportunity to live a normal and productive life because they have benefited from the life-sustaining technology commonly used in modern hospitals.

On the other hand, medical staffs in today's hospitals often have the technical ability to sustain biological life long after reasonable prospects for recovery are gone. Through the administration of artificial feeding and hydration, the lives of many terminal or permanently comatose patients can be maintained almost indefinitely. Currently in the United States 10,000 patients are institutionalized in irreversible comas and are being maintained through artificial means.

While modern science has extended life, it has also prolonged death. Numerous publicly reported cases have made this problem a matter of general knowledge and concern. The case of 21-year-old Karen Ann Quinlan, who collapsed into a coma on April 15, 1975, and remained on a respirator for one year, probably did more to alert the public to the dilemma of modern medicine than any case in recent years. More privately, many Christian families have faced the dilemma when called upon to make decisions regarding elderly parents and other loved ones who are "alive" only because the sound of a mechanical respirator or a dialysis machine says they are. Many people in America fear reaching the end of their lives hooked up to machines.

Christians who believe in the sanctity of life and who are faced with these circumstances face enormously difficult questions. What is life? When do artificial means cease to contribute to meaningful life? Under what conditions and by what moral and religious criteria can such support measures be terminated?

As of February 2000, physician-assisted suicide is the only legal form of euthanasia in the United States, although only in the state of Oregon. It is also legal in Australia and the Netherlands. However, in recent years books and manuals that tell how to enact euthanasia for oneself have become abundant.

Defining the Terms

Modern medicine has the ability to maintain the appearance of human life beyond reasonable expectations for qualitative recovery from illness. This has greatly accented questions regarding the moral acceptability of euthanasia, usually referred to as "physician-assisted suicide." The term comes from a Greek word meaning "good or easy death."

Physician-assisted suicide (some prefer to speak of "assisted dying" rather than "assisted suicide") generally refers to a practice in which the physician, upon the patient's request, provides a lethal dose of medication that the patient intends to use to end his or her life. While physician-assisted suicide is a form of euthanasia, it is not the same. In it the patient, not the physician, actually administers the lethal medication. In the more traditional meaning of euthanasia, a physician or someone else would act directly to end the patient's life.

The following are some other practices that should be distinguished from physician-assisted suicide:

- **Terminal sedation.** This is the practice of sedating a terminally ill, competent patient to the point of unconsciousness, then allowing the patient to die of his or her disease, of starvation, or of dehydration.
- **Withholding/withdrawing life-sustaining treatments.** When a competent patient makes an informed decision to refuse life-sustaining treatment, there is virtual unanimity in state law and in the medical profession that this wish should be respected.
- **Pain medication that may hasten death.** Often a terminally ill, suffering patient may require dosages of pain medication that impair respiration or have other effects that may hasten death. It is generally held by most professional societies, and supported in court decisions, that this is justifiable so long as the primary intent is to relieve suffering.[1]

Ethicists generally agree on the meaning of euthanasia. But they often disagree regarding its applied meaning. Should the term refer only to the *intentional* merciful termination of human life? Is it distinguishable from the act of *allowing* a terminally ill patient to die by withdrawing artificial feeding and hydration?

Some ethicists hold that since withdrawing treatment in terminal cases intentionally ends the life of a person, the action should be termed euthanasia. They say that allowing a patient to die *is* an action and not merely an omission of action. So by this definition, euthanasia would include both the intentional, merciful termination of life (called active euthanasia) *and* allowing to die (called passive euthanasia).

George Lundberg, M.D., editor of the *Journal of the American Medical Association,* accepts the broader definition and identifies six kinds of euthanasia:

- Passive, in which a physician may choose not to treat a condition secondary to a terminal patient's primary disease;
- Semipassive, in which a physician may withhold medical treatment, such as nutrition or fluids, from a person in irreversible coma;
- Semiactive, in which a physician may disconnect a ventilator from a patient who is in a stable but vegetative state;
- Accidental ("double effect"), in which a physician administers a narcotic to relieve pain in a terminally ill patient, but with the expected result that the narcotic will sufficiently depress respiration to bring on death;
- Suicidal, in which a person with a terminal illness intentionally takes his or her own life with an overdose of drugs, maybe provided by a physician;
- Active, in which a physician may administer a large, surely fatal overdose of morphine or potassium in a terminally ill patient.[2]

Other ethicists reject this broad definition of euthanasia. They insist that "allowing to die" and "euthanasia" *are not* the same. A meaningful and logical distinction must be made between "ceasing to employ extraordinary means to prolong life" and "euthanasia." Ethicists who support this position define euthanasia as the overt termination of a patient's life (either directly or assisted) when death is imminent. As the following diagram shows, they make a sharp distinction between euthanasia and the allowing to die.

As we discuss these topics, we will accept the more limited definition of euthanasia.

Currently in the United States physician-assisted suicide is legal only in the state of Oregon. Voters approved

Euthanasia

Voluntary Euthanasia*	Involuntary Euthanasia**

Allowing to Die

Voluntary Allowing to Die	Involuntary Allowing to Die

Voluntary*: the patient either makes or participates in the decision.

Involuntary**: a decision is made for the incapacitated patient.

the Oregon Death with Dignity Act in 1994. But a series of legal appeals postponed its implementation until October 27, 1997. The law made Oregon the first jurisdiction in the world to give physicians the legal permission to assist in the suicide of terminally ill patients. The Death with Dignity Act allows terminally ill Oregon residents to obtain from their physicians and to use prescriptions for self-administered, lethal medications. It states that ending one's life in accordance with the law does not constitute suicide.[3]

Many people applauded the "pioneering" role of the state in patient-directed medical practice and in ensuring death with "dignity." The law's practical focus is on permitting doctors to write a prescription for lethal medication. According to Courtney S. Campbell, "What follows such authorization is largely unregulated and ambiguous." Courtney cites the state's deputy attorney as acknowledging that the act is silent on many questions regarding implementation.[4]

Promoters and formulators of the Oregon Death with Dignity Act had three purposes in mind:

1. to provide terminally ill patients with the right to a "humane and dignified death" through ingestion of a lethal medication;

2. to provide physicians with immunity from legal
   and professional sanction for participating
   (whether by offering a diagnosis, providing information, or writing a prescription) in hastening patients' deaths; and
3. to assure the public that such a practice could be
   subject to regulation and public accountability (in
   contrast to the unregulated methods of Dr. Jack
   Kevorkian and the absence of accountability of
   physicians in the Netherlands).[5]

In 1999, 27 terminally ill Oregon residents committed
suicide with the help of lethal prescriptions from their
physicians. That number was up from 16 in 1998. Citing a
report in *The New England Journal of Medicine,* a story
in *USA Today* said that most of the persons who committed physician-assisted suicide in Oregon were well-educated, elderly cancer patients with health insurance who
were concerned about loss of autonomy, control of their
bodily functions, and physical suffering. Critics of the
state report said that it used bogus statistics to minimize
the importance of a human tragedy. Portland physician
Gregory Hamilton, head of Physicians for Compassionate
Care, complained that the report's authors surveyed only
the doctors who assisted in the suicides and purposely
overlooked known problems. Defenders of the report dis-
agreed and said that the report dispelled myths and dis-
proved the reasons behind the critics' opposition."[6]

As the Oregon law illustrates, many persons think
that euthanasia is a morally responsible option. An indi-
cation of just how strong the support is may be seen in
the response to *Final Exit,*[7] authored by Derek Humphrey
in 1991. Humphrey is the founder of the Hemlock Society.
Final Exit was written to replace *Let Me Die Before I
Wake.*[8] Printed in large type to assist persons with poor
eyesight, the book generated a storm of controversy. Several publishers refused it, and many people called for it to
be banned. It was on the *New York Times* best-seller list

for 18 weeks. Complete with details on ways to administer euthanasia, over 500,000 hardback copies were sold by the end of 1991. It became that year's fourth best-selling book in North America and was eventually translated into 10 languages. British publishers refused to issue *Final Exit*. But the imported American edition sold widely and openly. Increased in size, the book was reissued in 1992. *Final Exit* is only the best known of many books and manuals that instruct persons regarding euthanasia.

On October 27, 1999, the United States House of Representatives voted 271-156 in favor of the Pain Relief Promotion Act, which could undo Oregon's Death with Dignity Act. Supported by right-to-life groups and the American Medical Association, the bill would permit doctors to use federally controlled drugs, such as morphine, to relieve pain even if the unintended result is death. But it would not allow such prescriptions if the purpose of using them would be to cause death. The bill's backers said that it would encourage doctors to treat pain more aggressively.

Opponents of the House bill argued that it would have a "chilling effect" on doctors because they would fear being investigated. Barbara Coombs Lee, R.N., executive director of the Compassion in Dying Federation based in Portland, Oregon, said that the "bill will only make doctors overcautious and unwilling to aggressively treat their patients' pain."[9]

Allowing to Die

Prior to the recent explosive developments in medical technology the matter of allowing a terminally ill patient to die was relatively simple. The dying processes could not be fundamentally intercepted. Now, with the emergence of sophisticated life-support systems, Christians must make decisions about the termination of life. Many of us are unprepared.

Before the advent of the life-support systems that fill modern intensive care units, a doctor's or nurse's commit-

ment to do all within his or her power to save life meant
that if the efforts were successful, patients would likely
be restored to a significant measure of cognition, mobility, and productivity. Today the traditional commitment to
saving life presents painful ethical and emotional problems. Prolonging life for terminally ill persons by artificial
measures often raises serious questions about the morality of the measures themselves. Under what conditions
should sophisticated life-support procedures be employed? And when they are, when may they be discontin-
ued? Should mechanical ventilation be continued after
the quality of a patient's life has been severely and irre-
versibly compromised? Does a person have a right to die?

There is no uniform Christian appraisal of "allowing
to die." The technology that can add so much to medical
care can also place upon us tragic and painful decisions
regarding when to employ and when to stop using it.
Christians will make decisions based on deeply held convictions regarding the sanctity of human life. They should
know, however, that "allowing to die" lies quite within
the bounds of primary Christian values.

When death is eminent, or when a person is in a per-
sistent vegetative state, Christians can express their trust
in God by releasing life back into God's care and keeping.
They do not violate their faith in God by refusing to employ all that technology can provide. Nor do they show
any failure of love when they release a relative from aim-
less dependence on medical technology. Christians know
that their security rests in God's unfailing love, not in biological functions. Under certain circumstance Christians
can, as an exercise of their faith, relinquish their grip on
physical life. In that action they can express their trust in
the God from whom death cannot separate them. And
they can affirm their hope in the resurrection. As the
saints have known through the centuries, dying should
be a time when we affirm, "'Death is swallowed up in
victory.' 'O death, where is thy victory? O death, where is

thy sting?' . . . thanks be to God, who gives us the victory through our Lord Jesus Christ" (1 Cor. 15:54-57, rsv).

Euthanasia

Critical United States Supreme Court Decisions. In January 1997 the United States Supreme Court heard arguments *(Vacco v. Quill* and *Washington v. Glucksberg)* that pushed the question of the right to die to a different level. In these two cases the Court was asked to decide whether American citizens have a constitutional right to euthanasia, or more particularly, to physician-assisted suicide. Should doctors—forsaking the Hippocratic oath— be permitted to prescribe lethal doses of medication to help mortally ill patients end their lives (e.g., a 34-year-old lymphoma patient in excruciating pain)?

In the *Vacco v. Quill* case, Timothy E. Quill, along with other physicians and three seriously ill patients who have since died, challenged the constitutionality of New York State's ban on physician-assisted suicide. New York's ban, while permitting patients to refuse lifesaving treatment on their own, made it a crime for doctors to help patients commit or attempt suicide. This was true even of terminally ill patients who are in great pain.

The Supreme Court was asked to determine whether or not New York's ban violated the Fourteenth Amendment's Equal Protection Clause. New York allowed competent terminally ill adults to withdraw their own lifesaving treatment, but denied the same right to patients who could not withdraw their own treatment and could only hope that a physician would do this for them.

On June 26, 1997, the Supreme Court concluded that New York's ban on physician-assisted suicide was rationally related to the state's legitimate interest in protecting medical ethics. The ban protected the state's legitimate interest in preventing euthanasia and shielding the disabled and terminally ill from prejudice, which might encourage them to end their lives. Above all, the state's law protected its legitimate interest in preserving human life.

While acknowledging the difficulty of its task, the Court distinguished between *the refusal of lifesaving treatment* and *assisted suicide*. The Court noted that assisted suicide involves the criminal elements of causation and intent. No matter how noble a physician's motives may be, he or she may not deliberately cause, hasten, or aid a patient's death.

A Christian Appraisal of Euthanasia

Traditionally, Christians have opposed euthanasia because of their strong belief that God gives life to us. He alone has dominion over human life, and its termination is not our prerogative. Christians have held that euthanasia constitutes the sin of either murder if administered by a second party or suicide if administered by oneself.

The Bible records only one instance of active euthanasia, the "mercy killing" of King Saul by an unnamed Amalekite (2 Sam. 1:1-15). The one who administered euthanasia was himself immediately struck down at David's command. However, the execution occurred not primarily because of the *kind* of action but because of the one ("the LORD's anointed," v. 14) who was "euthanized." So the Bible gives us no direct guidance on this matter, except its insistence that human life is sacred and must not be violated.

The sixth commandment says, "You shall not murder." But the question arises, "Is euthanasia the same as violently and maliciously destroying the life of another?" Judged by intent and definition, it is not. By what principle, then, are Christians to be guided? Does euthanasia violate a reverence for the sanctity of life? Members of the Hemlock Society, who advocate the legalization of euthanasia, are prompted by humane and merciful interests. They believe that carefully monitored legalized euthanasia would demonstrate respect rather than disrespect for life.

Is There a Christian Case for Euthanasia?

It is unusual to find Christian ethicists and theologians who maintain that physician-assisted suicide, or any form of euthanasia, is compatible with the Christian faith. But some persons advance arguments in favor of physician-assisted suicide that claim Christian support. Let us examine their stance.

First, Christians believe that human life is not an end in itself. Therefore, it should not be held onto as those who do not share the Christian hope might do. As a result, Christian proponents of euthanasia believe they can actively terminate life within the bounds of Christian convictions and faith. Biological life isn't the basis for life's meaning, they say. Our relationships with God and others give life its meaning.

They conclude that taking from life its last drop of biological existence when death is imminent and life has become torturous demonstrates not faith and worship, but fear and faithlessness.

Second, Christians should not commit the error of worshiping technology instead of God. Medical technology can extend pointless existence for a long time. But there comes a time when it cannot promise any hope of returning us to appreciable health, and it cannot control pain and suffering. When this happens, trust in God as the One in whom we hope, not technology, should have the last word regarding whether we live or die.

Third, Christian proponents of euthanasia say that it does not deprive church members, family, and friends of the opportunity to show love, support, and the meaning of community. Hanging onto life when it is pointless to do so, they say, is itself selfish. Doing so, they believe, unnecessarily taxes the resources of families, friends, and congregations that could be put to much better use.

Fourth, in some instances in which death is imminent and the dying process is torturous, Christian proponents of euthanasia say it is morally permissible to intervene. They contend that euthanasia mercifully releases one from pointless suffering and thereby complies with Jesus' beatitude "Blessed are the merciful."

The fifth argument contends that since for Christians human life is of value because it is God's gift, and not because of its "usefulness," a Christian can under certain circumstances actively return the gift to God as a good steward.

Sixth, for some believers it seems that technology has taken control of the process of dying. To retrieve control of the death process and to curb the ever-increasing power of technology over our lives, these believers say that physician-assisted suicide could be a viable option.[10]

Finally, for advocates of euthanasia, the whole notion of identifying "assisted dying" with "suicide" is erroneous. One who commits suicide should not be compared to a terminally ill person whose death is imminent. The two actions, they say, involve two distinctly different moral situations and should be treated as such. The traditional arguments used to condemn suicide are not applicable to assisted dying, they claim.

The Christian Case Against Euthanasia

Overwhelmingly, Christian tradition has opposed euthanasia. Let us examine the major reasons.

First, Christians should pay careful attention to the long tradition of opposition to euthanasia that has characterized Church history. Therein we find the wisdom of the great teachers of the Church, who have carefully examined euthanasia in light of the Scripture and the content of our faith. "The Christian tradition has from early times consistently and unequivocally prohibited suicide, the intentional taking of one's own life."[11] Consistently, the Early Church fathers opposed euthanasia. The Early Church's prohibition against euthanasia has been upheld by Martin Luther, John Calvin, John Wesley, the Roman Catholics,[12] the

Greek Orthodox Church, the Russian Orthodox Church, the Lutheran Church (Missouri Synod), the Mennonite Church, and the National Association of Evangelicals.

Second, if God is the giver of human life and if we are stewards of God's gift, then to the very end we must treat life as the gift that it is. No Christian can abide by this principle and at the same time take control over the gift by deciding the time when life will end. Euthanasia aggressively seizes control over what one does not own. It breaks faith with God and throws the gift back into His face.

Christians must not be like secularists, who don't view human life as a gift from God. Christians don't think of life as gaining its meaning within the confines of this world. For Christians, the question "What should we do?" is preceded by "To whom to do we belong?" When that question is answered correctly, then the answer to the first question will rule out euthanasia for Christians.

Christians also know how easily human life can be cheapened and disregarded. We know how easily ruthless rulers can turn the powers of state against its own citizens. We know about Auschwitz and Treblinka. We observe how for the sake of monetary profit the most cherished values can be forced into slavery. We watch daily as the entertainment media cheapen family life, the unborn, and human sexuality. Euthanasia, too, will cheapen life's value in society at large. It sends a signal that human life is just one more disposable thing among others. Damaged? Worn out? Just dispose of it.

Euthanasia erodes the fragile yet fundamental respect for human life that makes the human community possible. Christians can bear witness to their respect for the human community by stating why they oppose euthanasia.

Third, it is true that many times suffering seems to serve no good purpose. But there are many times when through the way we respond to suffering, we can show our trust in the eternal God who suffers with us. How a

Christian bears physical suffering can demonstrate to others the power of God's grace and the meaning of faith and hope. Euthanasia abruptly cuts short any opportunity to know and bear witness to God's sustaining presence. Euthanasia terminates any possibility of making suffering redemptive and instructive.

Euthanasia contributes to our society's fixation on the absence of suffering as life's highest goal. Our society's addiction to the "quick fix," to pain relievers and to instant gratification, is hardly the model for Christian discipleship.

Fourth, euthanasia, including physician-assisted suicide, is selfish because it cuts a person off from the Christian community. As Christians we do not exist as lone individuals. Rather, we are members of Christ's body. We belong to each other as do the limbs of our bodies. In Christ's Church we learn what it means to be "in Christ" in community only, in the fellowship of the Holy Spirit. We minister to each other in community even as Christ gives himself to the Church. Euthanasia would deny to the members of Christ's body opportunity to minister to and to serve, and it would shut out the nurture that comes to us from our Christian brothers and sisters. Euthanasia may be acceptable to persons who are not members of Christ's Church, but it isn't acceptable for those who know themselves to be "members of one another."

Fifth, euthanasia steps over a line that should never be crossed. It is perhaps the ultimate expression of human arrogance. Euthanasia ignores the reality of original sin and humanity's propensity to claim more knowledge than is warranted. Christians, as well as many others, recognize the destructive results of human arrogance.

In spite of claims to the contrary, euthanasia takes us down a path that intensifies our culture's tendency to diminish the value of human life. Not accidentally, some of the most vocal opponents of euthanasia and physician-assisted suicide are severely disabled people. Courtney

Campbell has presented a powerful argument against
physician-assisted suicide. He notes,

> What many disabled people can see quite clearly
> . . . is that the legalization of assisted suicide puts us
> on a very slippery slope. Once society accepts certain
> people's "right" to be killed, those who are in similar
> situations [those who live with severe suffering and
> infirmities] will have to confront an implicit, perhaps
> explicit, question: Aren't you better off dead too?
> [They] will need to justify their continued existence
> to family, friends, doctors and medical insurers.[13]

Let no one doubt that significant voices in American
society might begin suggesting that disabled persons
could justifiably be terminated. In *Practical Ethics* (1979),[14]
Princeton University professor Peter Singer stated that
since children less than a month old have no human consciousness, parents of a severely disabled infant should be
allowed to euthanize the infant to end its suffering. Such
action could also increase the family's happiness. Many
would object that if we start to kill severely handicapped
infants we will end up threatening disabled adults. To
that objection Singer responds, "To allow infanticide before the onset of awareness . . . cannot threaten anyone
who is in a position to worry about it. Anyone able to understand what it is to live or die must already be a person
and [have] the same right to life as all the rest of us."[15]

Sixth, in some settings the death process happens in
a context of isolation, loneliness, and even alienation.
When relational bonds of the seriously ill, elderly, or disabled are absent, they may choose assisted suicide in a
spirit of despair. This is hardly a good reason to end one's
life. Rather than placing elderly and infirm persons in
such a position, we should offer them care, compassion,
and companionship.[16]

Finally, attempting to justify euthanasia because it
mercifully relieves suffering as nothing else can ignores the
medical community's increasing ability to "manage pain."

Leaders of the hospice movement, for example, have made major strides in pain management. Currently, the pain of many terminally ill patients is so poorly managed that it often makes euthanasia appear to be the only alternative to pointless suffering. Many patients spend their last days in needless agony, rather than in peace and comfort.

In recent years a model for treating persons with incurable diseases has gained widespread attention and favor. It is known as palliative care. Palliative care is "the active total care of patients whose disease is not responsive to curative treatment. Control of pain, of other symptoms, and of psychological, social and spiritual problems is paramount. The goal of palliative care is the achievement of the best possible quality of life for patients and their families."[17]

Palliative care has much in common with the hospice movement. But in the United States palliative care is evolving in a way that goes beyond the American version of hospice. Palliative care aims at addressing the physical, psychosocial, and spiritual concerns that contribute to both the quality of life and quality of dying for patients with life-threatening illnesses at any phase of the disease. Although the focus intensifies at the end of life, the core issues—comfort and function—defined broadly and evaluated within the context of the family, are important throughout the course of the disease.

The palliative care model recognizes the need to address symptom distress, physical impairments, psychosocial disturbances, and spiritual distress, even during the period of aggressive primary therapy. The foundation of palliative care is comprehensive assessment. In contrast to the traditional medical model, palliative care involves an ongoing consideration of interrelated problems that impact the individual and the family.

Advance Directives and Durable Power of Attorney[18]

"Advance directive" is a general term for the documents persons prepare and sign while they are mentally competent. Their purpose is to communicate health-care preferences a person wants others to observe when the primary party loses the capacity to make or communicate his or her own wishes and decisions.

The most important benefit of an advance directive is its value as a tool of communication. State laws authorize a person to name someone to make health-care decisions when the person cannot. In some contexts it also refers to living wills and the informal directives that people make in letters, conversations, and conduct.[19]

A "durable power of attorney" allows a person to appoint another to make health-care decisions for him or her when he or she is incapacitated. The document goes into effect only when the person involved cannot make or communicate decisions.

PART 3

Human Needs and Technical Resources

In the story of the Good Samaritan (Luke 10:25-37), the resources of the generous Samaritan adequately match the needs of the wounded man. So the question "What should be done for this man who has been attacked by robbers?" has a fairly simple answer.

But what if we were to vary the story? Suppose *five* men had been going from Jerusalem to Jericho, and the band of robbers had overpowered and seriously wounded all of them? Along comes the Samaritan with the same amount of resources as in the New Testament account. The needs obviously outstrip the available resources. *Now* what is the neighborly or just thing for the Samaritan to do? Who should he assist when he can't assist all five men, even though all five have needs? Love alone will not answer the question for the simple reason that external restraints beyond love's control have been placed upon the situation.

If the Samaritan is to act justly and as a good neighbor, he must now find access to defensible criteria of justice and fair distribution. When administering his criteria, he will not be able to satisfy all the requests for assistance. What will it now mean for the Samaritan to be a "good neighbor"?

The question must not be dismissed as a trivial one. In the world of biotechnology and its medical applications, identifiable human needs often outdistance available resources at numerous levels. Decision-makers in government, medicine, and insurance companies, as well as researchers and employers, must make discretionary decisions that leave some human needs unmet. Often as the level of medical technology becomes more sophisticated, the problem intensifies. Cost enters as a criterion for delineating between the "haves" and the "have nots." The distinction between social classes and nations surfaces. The distance between the availability of technical resources and human needs, and how to deal justly with the disparity, constitute a major topic in bioethics.

We turn now to a discussion of human needs and technical resources.

5

THE RIGHT TO HEALTH CARE

Two years ago Vanessa McCartney was diagnosed with breast cancer. She was not able to afford the care she needed, because she had joined the ranks of the uninsured—more than 44 million Americans who lack health insurance. At first she seemed an ideal candidate for beating cancer. She ate a healthful diet and didn't drink or smoke. Three of her grandparents had lived into their 80s. Vanessa had regularly seen a gynecologist until 1997 when her husband, Carl, lost his job in a small engineering firm.

Carl supported the family with a series of temporary, low-paying jobs. None of them provided health benefits. Consequently, the McCartneys used no medical services for more than three years. They were "outsiders" in the United States health-care system. They couldn't afford membership in the club. But neither could they afford to be outcasts.

In the summer of 1998 Vanessa began to experience increased fatigue and bone pain. But she had to forego medical treatment because she couldn't afford to pay a doctor. In October of that year Vanessa learned of a clinic where she could get a free examination. She did go, but it was too late—she already had advanced breast cancer.

Three weeks later, Vanessa was dead at age 36. She left behind three children, aged 9, 14, and 17. But the story did not end there. Staggered by the tragedy, Carl faced hospital bills of more than $40,000. Even though Carl earned only about $20,000 a year, he did not qualify for

Medicaid in New York. The unpaid bills forced the family into bankruptcy.

Vanessa's grieving mother, Brenda Ann Johnson, was puzzled over the justice of a health-care system that leaves many people unprotected from catastrophe: "In this country, where we have the best medical care in the world, it all seemed so unnecessary. It's like someone starving to death in the middle of a sumptuous banquet."

The Problem

Vanessa's story puts in sharp focus one of the most urgent and complex topics in bioethics—just access to health care.

The 20th century witnessed sweeping changes in the nature of health care in industrialized countries, and to a lesser extent in developing countries. But the medical wonders of the century were not equitably distributed. At no point is the gap between the "haves" and "have nots" more prominent. This is true inside and between nations. It is certainly true inside the United States.

Who in a society should benefit from high-tech medical care—those who can afford it or those most in need? And how is health care to be financed—by private insurance (which limits access) or at public expense? If these questions can be answered, there are more. What level of health care should a country guarantee? Should everyone have access to the ultimate in medical technology? If not, how are we to decide the minimally appropriate level of care to which a nation's populace should have access? Finally, what bearing, if any, should one's lifestyle have on one's access to limited medical resources?

The system of health care in place in a nation is an indicator of its culture, history, political structure, wealth, values, and traditions. Some countries establish central control over health care. This is known as a "closed" system, because there is a fixed national budget for health care. Some countries even provide a national health-care system, funded and administered by the government. Centralized systems attempt to establish a measure of equality in the distribution of facilities and health-care workers. Some centralized systems decide how many and what types (specialists) of doctors, nurses, and other health-care workers will be educated. Availability of health-care services for all persons is maintained at the expense of not giving potentially lifesaving services to a few. In practice, however, no countries are actually this egalitarian. The wealthy and well-placed find ways to receive better care than the average citizen.

Health care in the United States reflects a particular national history, social values, and political and economic structures that lead away from central health-care control. Our approach is known as an "open" system. There is no fixed national budget for health care. Instead, we have a patchwork system for financing health care, which makes it next to impossible to allocate resources rationally and equitably. This doesn't mean that our system is wrong—it simply recognizes that certain problems travel in its company.

The marketplace, not the federal government, has traditionally decided how many doctors and nurses (and in what specializations) will be educated. This has not always been generally beneficial for the American populace. As the practice of medicine and medical technology has become more sophisticated, there has been an increase in the number of specialists and a decreasing number of generalists. In 1950 nearly 50 percent of all physicians were generalists. In 1990 only 30 percent were generalists. The decline has probably contributed to the poor access to medical care by those in rural areas or in urban areas among those with low incomes.[1]

Contributing to the problem in the United States, as well as in other countries, are (1) the expense of new medical technology, (2) the rising cost of prescription medicines, and (3) the increasing longevity of older people who require more care. Additional factors combine to increase insurance premiums and to defeat the efforts of many employers to provide medical insurance for their employees.

There is a growing awareness that accelerating health-care costs come at the expense of other urgent social needs.[2] Deteriorating schools, homelessness, poverty, and combating crime receive less than adequate funding while inordinate amounts of the gross national product are being used to pay the high costs of health care.

Another part of the health-care problem is the growing evidence that a substantial number of medical care services may provide, at best, only marginal benefits. It is an illusion that increasing expenditures maximize benefits. Even though escalating costs and specialized benefits are the norm for developed countries, many developing and economically strapped countries can't offer their citizens even basic public health care (such as immunization and sanitation). In such instances, smaller outlays of money would yield much wider margins of benefit to a broader sector of society.[3]

Managed Care

By the early 1990s the rising costs of health care in the United States resulted in a revolution in how health-care services are provided and paid for. Instead of the federally managed health-care program (not nationalized medicine) President Bill Clinton proposed, the marketplace drove and decided the shape of reform. Beginning in the late 1970s and early 1980s, the traditional fee-for-service system, in which doctors and hospitals decided the costs and kinds of services to offer, began to be replaced by a system of managed-care organizations. These included health maintenance organizations (HMOs), preferred provider organizations, and several variations of these two.

Health-care providers went through tortuous adjustments to the new arrangements. Many doctors who had been accustomed to the old fee-for-service system left the practice of medicine. Nevertheless, managed care became a fact of life for American medicine. In 1992 HMOs covered 55 percent of American workers and their families. The percentage rose to 86 by 1998.[4]

However, before long Americans developed mixed feelings about the new medical revolution. Throughout the 1990s, battles raged over how well or how poorly the new structure was working. Many charged that the HMOs were much more interested in profits than in caring for their clients. Doctors maintained that the new structure had violated the sacred trust between them and their patients. The doctor, in consultation with his or her patient, could no longer alone decide the patient's care. Limits were placed on how long patients could remain in hospitals, and the HMOs set limits on what they would pay for hospital care. Suspicions mounted that the HMOs were eliminating from coverage those persons in the population who had complex and costly needs, such as quadriplegics.

Not surprisingly, in the latter part of the decade a nationwide backlash against the HMOs rolled across the United States. Fear that HMOs were placing monetary interests above patient care,[5] and fears that care would not be available when needed, made "managed care" an acronym "akin to scarlet letters for many consumers and doctors."[6]

Prescription Medicines

One of the most contentious elements in the battle over health care in the United States is the soaring cost of prescription medicine. At a time when in an aging population the demand for prescription drugs is growing, by one estimate drug prices have risen about 12.2 percent annually since 1993 (total health-care costs rose 5.1 percent).[7] The increases are particularly burdensome on the elderly, who spend three times as much on prescriptions as the rest of the population. In a report written by the

Health and Human Services Department, the Clinton Administration on April 4, 2000, accused drug companies of charging older Americans without health insurance 15 percent more for drugs than they charge insurance companies. As a result of the higher costs, in 1999 people without health insurance were five times more likely than those who have insurance to report that they had not taken the drugs they needed.[8]

A paradox of the American health-care system is that even though the United States invents most of the world's prescription drugs, thousands of Americans cross into Canada and Mexico to buy identical life-improving, death-defying drugs significantly more cheaply than they can in the United States.[9] As the year 2000 opened, a number of states were trying to find ways to regulate costs of pharmaceuticals within their jurisdictions.

An Uncertain Future

As the new millennium began, there was heated debate in the United States over how to address the problem of skyrocketing health-care costs and what to do about the uninsured. No social or political consensus regarding solutions existed.[10]

What will be left standing when the dust settles? At this point no one knows. Experts in the field recognize that the revolution in health care and health-care coverage is still occurring. Early into the year 2000, opinions were sharply divided over the future of HMOs. Some observers believed that as the HMOs mature they will improve their quality of service. According to this estimate, despite the challenges, the demand for health plans such as the HMOs will likely endure. Analysts who support the positive assessment think that HMOs can still reinvent medical practice and provide the best care for even the sickest patients.

Others are sure that, left to themselves, the HMOs cannot and will not correct problems and abuses. They say that since they need to be profitable, they are caught in a conflict of interest they cannot resolve alone. Resolution will come, some analysts say, through federal oversight. One critic of the new system, Jane Bryant Quinn, says that the United States is on the verge of "rationed care." The options are either to pay more for medical coverage or to limit care in more aggressive ways.[11]

As the year 2000 got underway, a much more ominous assessment of the HMOs was gathering steam. "An emerging consensus among some medical economics experts is that the managed-care concept is doomed."[12] The principal reason for this negative assessment is an accelerating loss of profitability for the HMOs, a problem technically known as "high medical loss ratio."

Other observers maintain that the uncertainties surrounding managed care should teach us a lesson. A solution to the dilemma lies neither in increased payments for health care by employers or employees, nor in severely rationed care. Instead, they say, the responsibility for basic health-care insurance lies with the federal government. Froma Harrop asks, "Why can't this nation get its act together and guarantee basic coverage for everyone?"[12]

Obviously, hard choices lie ahead. The simple fact is that health care is not a nation's, an employer's, or a family's only moral responsibility or good to be considered.

Increased tensions will occur between the autonomous desires and "needs" of individuals and pressures to limit the range of health care. Perceived infringements on personal freedoms and "rights" to health care will occur.

Rationing Health Care

Many observers believe that in one form or another America will have to accept health care rationing. Bioethicist John F. Kilner defines rationing as distributing health-care resources in ways that leave "certain people without some form of potentially beneficial health care, at least temporarily and against their wishes."[14] He says that rationing is inevitable. In fact health-care rationing in some forms already exists. Demands outstrip resources, and so selective distribution is necessary. Additional reasons for rationing are that health-care reform will make the situation worse. Our focus on acute care—on curing—has come at the expense of adequate funding for preventive research and medicine, long-term care, and palliative care. Also, the increasing availability and expense of medical technology will demand some form of rationing.[15]

Toward Just Access to Health Care

If Christians are truly convinced regarding the inviolable value of all persons, then they cannot sit idly by while many persons are left out of access to basic health care while others benefit from extensive access. Admittedly, this is a most difficult problem. It is difficult to address within the confines of one's own country, and even more so when one tries to think and act with a sense of global responsibility. There is no easily identifiable boundary between a responsible desire for health-care resources and selfishness. We can say, however, that an insatiable desire to draw upon medical resources for oneself or one's family attaches more importance to physical life than Christians should ever be guilty of.

Tom Beuchamp and James Childress present two arguments that support a universal right to health care. Both arguments find support in the twin Christian convictions discussed earlier: "the inviolable value of the person" and "social solidarity."

The two arguments they identify are (1) an argument from collective social protection and (2) an argument from fair opportunity. The first compares health needs and other needs. Just as a person has a right for collective protection against crime, fire, and a polluted environment, even so a person has a right to collective protection against preventable diseases and poor public sanitation and to primary health care. Essential health-care services should be a collective responsibility. The support for universal health care in a society by comparison to other fundamental rights appeals to coherence: "If government has an obligation to provide one type of essential service, then it must have an obligation to provide another."[16]

The second argument for a decent minimum of health care rests on an appeal to fairness. In the interest of justice, a society has a responsibility to counteract a lack of opportunity brought on by misfortune. Persons have no meaningful control over misfortune. "A society cannot discharge its obligation under the fair-opportunity rule without fairly allocating health care resources. All citizens have a right to the resources correlative to this social obligation."[17]

Basic health care should not depend on where a person is on the scale of wealth or social influence. To think that access to basic health care is a privilege that one must earn through wealth and social position violates the Christian convictions of the inviolable value of the person and social solidarity. The prophet Micah pronounced God's judgment on the social elites who thought their positions of social privilege justified the less-than-human conditions of those far below them on the social ladder. And in Matthew 25, Jesus destroyed the notion that the lack of social standing justifies treating some people as less than the objects of God's care and visitation. In calling for minimal universal health care, Beauchamp and Childress do not mean to suggest a uniform distribution of health-care resources. They believe that a two-tiered system of health is morally defensible. *Tier One:* a society such as the United States ought to insure that the basic and catastrophic health care needs of all citizens are met. *Tier Two:* voluntary private coverage for other health-care needs and desires would be available. In the first tier, distribution of health care would be based on primary needs.[18] In the second tier, better services would be available for purchase at personal expense.[19]

A major obstacle to establishing the first tier is the difficulty of defining "decent minimum health care" in functional terms.[20] An additional problem is whether or not a careless person should forfeit his or her right to health care. Should a woman who has smoked for 40 years, knowing of its risks and who now has lung cancer, forfeit her right to minimal health care?

A Challenge for Christians

Our world requires an ethic that can promote a sense of community and responsibility. It must be one that transcends the social, racial, and national ghettos that wall off basic health care to many while permitting the luxury of health care for others. Jesus' story of the Good Samaritan (Luke 10:25-37) should illustrate for us the sin of permitting one's own social boundaries to decide the worth of those beyond the boundaries. Unlike the priest and the Levite, the Good Samaritan transcended the narrow definitions of "neighbor" that had been handed him at birth.

Will we Christians offer to the world a model of "neighborliness" that passes beyond selfishness and market-driven evaluations of persons? Will we demand better than "privilege" of our governments? To follow Christ, we must not be deceived by a consumer-defined culture that cares nothing for the kingdom of God.

On a larger scale, Christians in developed countries cannot answer these questions for themselves while ignoring the desperate state of health care in many developing countries. We must not horde exotic medical resources while ignoring the death of many in poor countries due to diseases that first world countries eliminated long ago.

6

HUMAN EXPERIMENTATION

On September 17, 1999, Jesse Gelsinger died. Jesse was an 18-year-old from Tucson, Arizona, who suffered from an inherited liver disorder. He had volunteered to participate in a gene-therapy study at Penn State University that involved injecting a cold virus carrying healthy genes directly into the liver's main artery. The virus, called adenovirus, is believed to have triggered a chain of events that led to his death. Adenovirus has been the most commonly used vehicle for delivering genes in gene-therapy experiments.[1]

Jesse's death prompted an investigation by the United States Food and Drug Administration, who, on December 8, 1999, accused scientists at Penn State of violating gene-therapy study regulations that might have prevented the young man's death.[2] Jesse was enrolled in the study despite abnormal liver enzyme levels. His condition should have excluded him from participating in the research project. Further investigation revealed that the established mechanisms meant to protect subjects who participate in investigational drug studies were ignored time and time again. The investigators failed to notify the FDA of several problems that arose during the study. If the problems had been disclosed, the research would have been terminated.

James Chapman, assistant professor and chairman of the chemistry department at Rockhurst University in Kansas City, says that the institutional review board erred. A review examines research proposals for risks to the persons who will participate. The research guidelines are supposed to inform participants of the risks associated with the research. In this case the informed consent guidelines were "riddled with omissions." The death of Jesse Gelsinger occurred because some "researchers were unwilling to comply with the regulation imposed upon them by the FDA." Chapman adds that even after Jesse's death, some biotechnology companies were meeting with federal officials in an attempt to reduce the regulations that govern the disclosure of information given to the public.[3]

The tragic story of Jesse Gelsinger vividly portrays how human carelessness, even the self-interests of researchers, can harm the very people human experimentation is meant to help. The story issued a wake-up call to scientists, politicians, and biotech firms that stand to make large profits from the results of human experimentation. Jesse's unnecessary death is a stark reminder of the "myth of objectivity" in scientific research. Ulterior motives can cause research to race ahead of moral constraints. This particular death reminds us that only the presence of strict moral, professional, and governmental responsibility can steer the use of science in the humane directions we really want to go.

However, as tragic and irresponsible as Jesse's death was, it does not diminish the need for medical research that uses persons as subjects. Chapman's stern criticism of the Jesse Gelsinger case nevertheless includes an endorsement of human research for making advances in medicine and biotechnology. But moral issues are far more urgent than making medical advances available to the public.

Fetal Tissue Research

On Wednesday, January 29, 1997, after extensive laboratory research and two years of ethical debate, University of Chicago surgeons moved further into a new area of research known as fetal tissue research. The surgeons

transplanted retinal cells from an aborted fetus into the
eye of an 80-year-old woman. They hoped that their actions would eventually lead to curing the leading cause of
blindness (macular degeneration of the retina, a mysteri-
ous disorder that afflicts as many as 15 million Americans, with 200,000 new cases yearly) in an aging U.S.
population. In the delicate two-hour operation, retinal
surgeon Samir Patel inserted a pinhead-sized dot of tissue containing about 250,000 fetal cells under the damaged area of the woman's left retina. The cells were collected from the eyes of a fetus donated by the mother
after she underwent an abortion to save her life.[4]

The experiment in Chicago is but an instance of one
of the most controversial, and many say most promising,
aspects of experimentation on humans. Fetal tissue
means any organ or part of the fetus, including the umbil-
ical cord and placental blood or tissue. Fetal tissue research is attractive principally because fetal tissue has
unique properties that make it less likely to be rejected
when transplanted.

The use of transplanted fetal tissue could have a major
impact on the treatment of diabetes, multiple sclerosis,
leukemia, immune disorders, and several neurological diseases, including Parkinson's, Huntington's, and
Alzheimer's. Fetal liver tissue might be used to treat
leukemia, aplastic anemia, inherited metabolic disorders,
and radiation injuries. Fetal neural tissue might even lead
to successfully treating types of vision impairment and
spinal cord injuries. Christine Gorman reported in May
2000 that researchers have so far "offered promises aplen-
ty about what stem cells can do but very little proof."[5]

But in Roger Pederson's lab at the University of California in San Francisco, he has managed to turn a group
of stem cells (progenitor cells) into a patch of thriving,
beating cardiac muscle. "It's amazing," Pedersen says,
when you put unspecified cells away, come back after the
weekend, and there's a clump of heartlike cells beating

before your eyes in a dish." For now, embryonic stem cells seem to have the greatest potential for "medical miracles." Stem cells derived from embryos have the potential to become just about anything—from teeth to muscle to neurons. They are primed to differentiate.[6]

The controversies surrounding the use of fetal tissue in research involve ethical, legal, social, and religious issues. Since this technology may likely affect many of us, we need to be alert to the concepts involved and the ethical questions that arise.

Undifferentiated stem cells taken from fetal tissue might in the future become the source of the most powerful treatments ever for degenerative diseases. Patient advocacy groups, such as the Juvenile Diabetes Foundation, Paralyzed Veterans of America, and some important members of the United States Congress support fetal tissue research. Opponents, including religious groups and many members of Congress, think that using cells from fetal tissue for research is immoral because harvesting them destroys the embryos. Critics say that destruction of human embryos—no matter what the reason—is abhorrent. Janet Parshall, for example, chief spokesperson for the Family Research Council, said, "I think it's the worst kind of utilitarianism."[7]

Eric Meslin, a member of the National Bioethics Advisory Commission, said that the panel thought the potential the research holds for treating diseases such as Alzheimer's and Parkinson's outweigh the stated ethical concerns. He recommended that only spare human embryos donated by fertility clinics (only embryos that are "in excess of clinical use," that is, left over from couples via fertility clinics) could be used in federally funded research. Couples must provide consent and have no financial incentive to donate the excess embryos for research. The recommendation was not to permit federally funded scientists to use embryos that were created specifically for research purposes.

Pluripotent stem cells are self-replicating. So researchers can create many, many cells from a single source. For research purposes, new embryos are not needed for each new experiment.

Fetal tissue research and its application poses ethical quandaries for scientists because of its association with the abortion debate. Persons who are opposed abortion on request fear that fetal tissue research will encourage abortions and even lead to illegally selling aborted embryos. The danger would accelerate if fetal tissue transplantation were to prove successful.

Opponents should not be dismissed as fools. In January 2000 a story surfaced that the University of Nebraska Medical Center in Omaha had established a relationship with an abortion clinic to supply aborted fetuses as sources of fetal stem cells. Dennis Smith, president of the University of Nebraska, defended the arrangement as the practice of academic freedom: "We can't teach or do research based on what an interest group wants us to do."[8]

We should note that in the Canadian discussion of fetal tissue research, questions have focused on commercialization of this and other forms of organ donation, rather than upon the morality of abortion.[9]

In January 1995, the Ramsey Colloquium, sponsored by the Institute on Religion and Public Life, issued a judgment regarding human embryo research. A panel of 19 experts had recommended to the National Institutes of Health that government funds should sponsor research on human embryos. It recommended that human embryos could be created in the laboratory for the sole purpose of using them as materials for research. In their response to the panel's recommendations, 26 Jewish and Christian theologians issued their critique of the panel's recommendations.[10] They condemned embryo research carried out on embryos created for research purposes as "morally repugnant." Conceiving embryos for this purpose "entails a grave injustice to innocent human beings, and constitutes

an assault upon the foundational ideas of human dignity
and rights essential to a free and decent society."[11] The
moral question posed by a human embryo is not whether it
is "protectable" but whether "it is in need of protection."

The moral objections the Ramsey Colloquium issued
were directed toward research on embryos created
specifically for research purposes. The 1999 National Institutes for Health guidelines prohibit creating embryos
for research purposes.

Conclusion

While keeping in mind the possible hazards of human experimentation, we may still conclude that if medical science is to advance against disease and illness,
then research on human subjects will be necessary. The
ability to identify the causes of diseases and to develop
cures for them is a gift from God. The gift can be used in
a manner that actually brings glory to the Creator. But
Christians should insist on justifiable criteria and carefully monitored standards for all human experimentation.

7

THE ALLOCATION OF SCARCE MEDICAL RESOURCES

On December 27, 1999, at the University of Alberta Hospital in Edmonton, Ray Nelson received a new heart. Nelson, who used to swim 50 laps a day, received his new heart from a 55-year-old donor. Normally, because of its advanced age, the donor's heart would not have been used.

In 1998 Nelson underwent bypass surgery. But in September 1999 he was admitted to the hospital because of complications. Ten days after his transplant, Nelson was sitting up and talking.

So far this story seems fairly normal by today's transplant standards. What makes it highly unusual is that Ray Nelson is 79 years old, 14 years older than the maximum age for a transplant in Canada.

The heart transplant for Ray Nelson provoked an intense debate in Canada over whether the action was morally defensible. Technically, the transplant seemed to be successful. But that's not the point. The debate is about a just and fair allocation of scarce medical resources, in this case transplantable organs. In Canada where fewer than 200 heart transplants occur each year, as many as 6,000 Canadians are considered possible candidates. Given the large number of younger candidates and the high cost of a heart transplant ($150,000-250,000), how could anyone justify Nelson's new heart? How could the Canadian doctors and officials who made the decision justify their use of such a rare resource. Nelson had already lived an active 79 years.

Should society say to the Ray Nelsons, "Sorry, but given the scarcity of medical resources, it is wrong to transplant a heart (or some other transplant) into your chest. Why should you receive this scarce resource just so that you live a few more years?" Should not Nelson have just faced up to his own finitude? Should he have looked at the ways the money spent on him could be used more beneficially, and said no to the heart transplant?

Or, as some suspect, did Nelson succeed in unfairly manipulating the decision-making process? Did he use wealth and influence to secure an unjust advantage? If he had, he would have been neither the first nor the most famous to do so. Douglas Kinsella, a lecturer on medical ethics at the University of Calgary in Alberta, raised this question regarding Nelson's heart transplant.[1]

✳ ✳ ✳

On October 13, 1994, Contrenia Harrell cradled and caressed her tiny child, Stephanie. Stephanie became known nationwide as Baby K. The infant was born in Fairfax Hospital in Falls Church, Virginia, with most of her brain missing. On October 13 Baby K was about to celebrate her second birthday. Contrenia was going to throw a birthday party, complete with balloons, cake, candles, and hats. To her mother, the fact that Stephanie had lived for two years was already confirmation of a miracle. "Some thought she would die in a few hours, a few days, a few months. God's proven them wrong." Now Contrenia was awaiting "a total miracle." She was waiting for God to heal Stephanie so that she "could eventually grow up and play like other children."

Baby K was born with anencephaly, a condition in which the embryologic closure of the neural tube never completes, leaving the embryo to develop without the upper portion of its skull. A major portion of the brain does not develop. About 1,000 babies are born with anencephaly each year. Baby K had only a brain stem, a condition that is usually fatal in the first moments or days after birth. She could not think, hear, or feel. Until fitted with a respirator, she suffered three respiratory arrests that required intensive, costly hospital care.

Generally, all other parts of the infant's body are normal, which makes the organs candidates for transplantation. If the medical community waits until the infant dies, then the organs will likely not be useful for transplantation. They deteriorate in the death process.

For persons in medical and educational circles "the two-year" point marked an unresolved battle between the hospital and the mother. For them, Baby K was not a child, not a person "awaiting a miracle of healing." Baby K was a "living corpse." "This infant is not now a person, and won't become one," said Steven Luper-Foy, a philosophy professor at Trinity University and a member of a hospital bioethics committee in San Antonio. "It's like keeping alive a corpse."

While some parents have sought to donate organs of their anencephalic infants, Harrell fought to keep Baby K alive. The father (the couple never married and ceased living together) sided with the hospital. Said Contrenia, "He lacks faith."

Falls Church Hospital officials believed that continuing to provide extraordinary measures to prolong the dying process was medically and morally indefensible. So the hospital asked the federal courts for permission to refuse treatment. On July 1, 1993, a judge ruled that the hospital had a duty to provide full care. The court's decision marked the first case of anencephaly to be decided under the Emergency Medical Treatment and Active Labor Act. The act requires hospitals to treat any person with an emergency medical condition. It was also "the first time a court has ever ordered physicians to render medical care over their protests," said Stephan Lawton, an American Academy of Pediatrics lawyer.

At age two Stephanie's hospital bill totaled $247,872. The amount was paid in full by Harrell's insurer. Other bills were paid by Medicaid.[2]

One solution to the debate over transplanting the organs of anencephalic infants is to declare that they were never alive. Removing the organs while the infant is still breathing would maximize the likelihood that the infant's organs would be successfully transplanted and made to serve in a beneficial, redemptive manner.[3]

By what criteria should questions such as these be answered? Which decision would be consistent with Christian values, and which would best demonstrate stewardship of public resources? How are we to balance Ray Nelson's and Baby K's interests against the possible use of those funds to procure better textbooks for inner-city children, one project on which the thousands of dollars needed for Baby K could otherwise be spent? These questions are part of the broader question, How may we allocate scarce medical resources in ways that are both just and merciful?

The Problem

Ray Nelson and Baby K introduce us to one of the most baffling moral dilemmas the revolution in biotechnology has generated. How should those who are responsible for procuring and distributing scarce medical resources decide who should receive them when there are not enough to satisfy all of the needs?

Potentially limitless demands stand in sharp contrast to very limited supplies. While this is not a new problem, it has become significantly more difficult in the contemporary setting. Medical resources that often become scarce include expensive equipment and medicine, highly specialized practitioners, donors for organ transplant operations, and research facilities. The problem should be seen against the backdrop of skyrocketing costs for medical services that place individuals, governments, employers, hospitals, and insurance companies in bewildering situations.

Macroallocation/Microallocation

The task of allocating limited medical resources is extremely complex. Doing so in a society involves far more than moral considerations. Additional deciding factors include social values and histories, economics, international relations and commitments, and the political possibilities in a society at any given period. The health of the citizenry is important, but it must not receive more attention than is warranted. Physical health should not be worshiped. Aesthetic, education and science, and a nation's infrastructure also serve vital dimensions of the human community and spirit. Enriching culture is society's overall goal, and this demands wholeness of vision and purpose. Culture, Alfred N. Whitehead reminded us, is "activity of thought and receptiveness to beauty and humane feeling."[4]

The task of fairly dividing the social budget is usually classified according to two broad categories: *macroallocation* and *microallocation*. The second category has to be divided into three subproblems.

Macroallocation is the process of determining which sectors of a society will receive what portions of that society's limited resources. What portion of the national resources should go for health care? What portion should be committed to serve other social values? The other values include education, the arts, and the infrastructure (roads, waterways, etc.). No satisfactory moral formula exists for making this decision. Nor can the decisions be made simply on moral grounds. Also, the criteria for making the macrodecisions shifts from one national circumstance to another. No fixed line exists. Nor are the decisions neat ones. Such questions immediately put us in the arena of public policy.

Microallocation is the process of seeking just distribution once macroallocation has been determined. Assuming that the macrodecisions have been made, then another step must be taken. First, a society must decide how the portion allocated to health care will be distributed. The formal principle is that the allocations should be assigned in ways that best promote the health of a nation's citizens.

Once we have decided how much to spend on direct medical services, we must then decide who should receive those services and who should be denied them. Should Ray Nelson receive a new heart? How much of the limited resources should be used to keep Baby K alive? We cannot escape the question, "Who will live when not everyone can live?" In the 1960s and 1970s this question was dramatically illustrated by the allocation of renal dialysis machines. Access to these machines was a matter of life and death for many people. Some persons received treatment and returned to productive lives; others did not. They died.

Organ and Tissue Transplantation

The problem of microallocation is most acute in the area of organ and tissue transplantation. It has been referred to as a "conundrum without end."[5]

The new technology of organ transplantation is a procedure that has transformed medicine from an enterprise that works with the human body as is into a dynamic one capable of introducing new organs in place of faulty ones that endanger a person's life. What in the 1950s was highly experimental has now become one of the major success stories of modern medicine.

Currently there exists in the United States a severe shortage of organs for transplant. An average of 12 patients per day die while waiting for hearts, livers, or other organs. Between 1989 and 1999 the number of organ transplants in the United States doubled, but the waiting list tripled. Because of major advances in transplant technology, more patients are being referred for transplants, including many persons who likely would not have been placed on a list of transplant candidates.

The success of organ transplantation accelerated after 1979 with the introduction of the antirejection drug cyclosporine. As the practice of organ transplants accelerated in the United States, a heated controversy developed over the most equitable way to allocate and distribute transplantable organs. Should the allocation of transplantable organs be decided on a regional basis? Federal rules gave local patients priority when an organ became available. If no one locally was suitable, then recipients were sought regionally, then nationwide. Where one lived could be more important than how sick he or she was. The nation was divided into 63 local and 11 regional organ sectors. When an organ became available, priority was given to patients in the same local area.

If no local patients were suitable, then the United Network for Organ Sharing (UNOS), a nonprofit organization that operates the National Organ Procurement and Transplantation Network for the United States Department of Health and Human Services, searched for a suitable recipient in the region where the organ was donated. If no one suitable for the transplant could be found in that region, then UNOS looked at patients on waiting lists in the rest of the country. Under that system, UNOS reported, in 1998 the median waiting times for liver transplant patients were 439 days in the Baltimore area but only 147 days in nearby Washington, D.C. In New York City, the median wait was 511 days; across the river in New Jersey, it was 56 days.[6]

Some people waited for months and even years for organs. Some sought spots on lists at transplant centers throughout the country, where they pay to fly and perhaps pay for some or all of the operation. That is expensive and difficult for someone in grave medical condition.

The United States Department of Health and Human Services was concerned that doctors sometimes pick their own relatively healthy patients over very sick patients in hospitals across town or in another state.

In an effort to achieve a more equitable distribution, the United States Department of Health and Human Services (DHHS) in February 1998 set out to change the old system of organ distribution. Donna Shalala, secretary of the DHHS, announced plans to issue a set of rules aimed at helping the sickest patients first, regardless of where they live. In a letter to 89 members of Congress, Shalala wrote, "We have not achieved equitable distribution to those with greatest medical need." The goal of the proposed rules would be that when a person signs up for an organ transplant, the organ would come to the person in need rather than the person having to find an organ and fly to it.

Campbell Gardett, spokesperson for the DHHS, said, "We want to get the balance right."[7]

However, the intentions of the DHHS were not uniformly applauded. Numerous voices were raised in defense of the older system. Teresa Shafer of Fort Worth, Texas, for example, executive vice president of LifeGift Organ Donation Center of West Texas, which has offices in Amarillo and Lubbock, said her organization "is not in favor of one big waiting list" for organs. "Our transplant goal is to save the most people, and it is most efficient when done locally. It's the community taking care of the community."[8]

Death, Brain Death, and Organ Donation

A major moral question posed by transplanting organs revolves around the status of the person donating the organ. In some instances such as donating a kidney, a family member or friend may donate one of his or her kidneys. He or she will then go on living a normal life. But in other instances the donor must be recognized as dead before his or her organs can be justifiably transplanted. The organs of one person should not be harvested if he or she is still alive. And no one should be allowed to intentionally sacrifice his or her life (let alone the life of another) to provide organs for others.

But when is a person dead? Does harvesting the organs from "brain dead" donors constitute killing the donors, or are they in fact dead? There is general consensus among ethicists and persons in the legal and medical professions that harvesting organs from someone who has been declared "brain dead" does not constitute killing. Most professionals believe that brain death really is death.

The brain stem is a small region at the base of the brain. Its functioning is a necessary condition for biological life. It controls and integrates the body's biological functions, including breathing. The brain stem is also a necessary condition for personal human life, because a functioning brain stem is necessary for the capacity for consciousness. Once the brain stem shuts down, it does not revive.

However, there are those who argue that harvesting organs from donors or persons whose hearts are still beating (such as victims of severe head injuries whose vital functions are for a while kept going by artificial respiration, nutrition, and hydration but whose brains, including their brain stems, are permanently destroyed) does in truth kill a dying, but nonetheless living person. The "brain death" criterion, opponents say, permits removal of organs from living persons, not from already "dead" persons.[9]

As with any legitimate effort to improve the quality of human life, organ transplant technology has been used in immoral ways. One of the most morally repugnant abuses of transplant technology that has occurred, and still occurs, is black market trafficking in human organs. For years there have been rumors and reports of black market procurement and sale of human organs. The sinister practice seems particularly to exploit children in developing countries. After an article appeared in *Guardian Weekly* (September 30, 1990), titled "Brazilian Children Sold for Transplants," Amnesty International and Save the Children in Denmark began investigations.

At least some parents in developed nations who are desperate to save their child tend not to ask questions about the organ's origin. Amnesty International discovered that "people who travel for various organizations in the suspected countries say that trafficking in children who are sold so that their organs can be used for transplantation is well known and is a highly profitable black market business. But it is so devious that it is impossible to catch the people involved. It is also very dangerous to reveal information." A European Parliament committee in 1993 stated that "to deny the existence of such trafficking is comparable to denying the existence of the ovens and gas chambers during the last war."

As a consequence of the investigations and increased public awareness, there is closer cooperation between transplant centers to ensure that the organs each center receives have been obtained according to rigorous guidelines.[10]

In April 1996 the University of California at Berkeley conducted a conference titled "Commerce in Organs: Culture, Politics, and Bioethics in the Global Market." In announcing the conference, the university released the following statement:

> There has been a decade of spirited debate over a new transnational commerce in human organs—kidneys, corneas, liver tissue, and heart valves—to facilitate transplantation. In India, kidneys are sold on the open market through newspaper ads placed by doctors looking for healthy, living donors. In South Africa, the cadavers of poor, mostly Black, victims of urban violence are sometimes "looted" for usable organs. In China, the bodies of executed prisoners are

used to supply fresh organs. The sale of human organs for transplantation is a source of terror in shantytowns worldwide.

Such practices have been condemned by many international medical and human rights organizations, but not by professional societies of transplant specialists.[11]

PART 4

Changes in Life at Its Origin

Up to this point, we have examined medical technologies that affect persons in the condition medical and research science find them. Now we encounter an initially bewildering list of technologies that have the capacity to transcend the bounds of the given human genetic and reproductive limitations. In many respects the changes in human life that these developments anticipate bring with them the promise of great benefit to persons in all parts of the world. On the other hand the developments touch life at such fundamental levels they have generated calls for great caution if not an abrupt change in direction. We have arrived at the place at which we can alter the fundamental building blocks of life. How ought we to proceed from here?

The burgeoning technologies with which we will deal have profound implications for the family, community, agriculture, business, the nature and delivery of health care, the environment, and even the general characteristics of society itself. They confront the Christian faith with profound and wide-ranging moral questions.

In its 1982 report, the President's Commission for the Study of Ethical Problems in Medicine and Biomedical and Behavioral Research said, "The recently acquired capability to manipulate the genetic material of all living things is an important—even revolutionary—advance in the trajectory of human knowledge. But like revolutionary insights of the past that enriched understanding, it also unsettles notions that once seemed fixed and comfortable."[1]

The president's commission undertook its study in response to a request addressed to the president of the United States on June 20, 1980, by the general secretaries of the National Council of Churches, the Synagogue Council of America, and the United States Catholic Conference. That request said in part,

> We are rapidly moving into a new era of fundamental danger triggered by the rapid growth of genetic engineering. Albeit, there may be opportunity for doing good; the very term suggests the danger. Who shall determine how human good is best served when new life forms are being engineered? Who shall control genetic experimentation and its results which could have untold implications for human survival? Who will benefit and who will bear any adverse consequences, directly or indirectly?[2]

Christian denominations—and even Christians within denominations—offer diverse assessments of the practical applications given the new genetic and reproductive technologies. In the spring of 1987, the Roman Catholic Church in a landmark statement titled "Instruction on Respect for Human Life in Its Origin and on the Dignity of Procreation" condemned as immoral the use of new reproductive technologies such as artificial insemination (with rare exceptions allowed), in vitro fertilization, surrogate parenting, and prenatal diagnosis for the purposes of destroying a malformed fetus. The document opposes any attempt to overcome infertility through technologies that transcend normal sexual intercourse between husband and wife. Quoting from Pope John Paul II, the document says that these techniques expose humankind "to the temptation to go beyond the limits of a reasonable dominion over nature."

Protestants, on the other hand, present no such uniform response to reproductive technologies. There seem to be almost as many viewpoints as there are denominations.[4]

8

GENETIC RESEARCH AND GENETIC THERAPY

In the 1997 film *Gattaca*, it had become possible through genetic engineering to produce a class of genetically superior persons. The old bases for discrimination—race and ethnicity—had been replaced by a person's genetic structure. In the world that *Gattaca* describes, persons conceived naturally now occupied the lowest level on the social scale. They cleaned the toilets and polished the marble floors in the homes of the people at the top. The elite were those whose parents selected their traits from a library of genes. These persons received the highest opportunities for success and reaped the richest social benefits. The film declares, "Your genes are your résumé."

Admittedly, the film pushes the field of genetics into the realm of fantasy and entertainment. Nevertheless, it succeeds in calling attention to an astonishing revolution in genetics that began in earnest in the middle of the 20th century. Today, developments in genetics occur so rapidly that most of us have no hope of remaining abreast of what is going on. Tim Friend is correct: "Science races ahead like a bullet train, arriving at the station often far ahead of the understanding of its implications. Gene discoveries now are being made almost daily."[1]

The pace at which developments in genetic research are occurring is stunning. Not until 1953 did American geneticist James Watson and British biophysicist Francis Crick, building on the work of Maurice Wilkins, discover the molecular structure of DNA. For their accomplishment, the three men received the 1962 Nobel Prize for Physiology or Medicine. Only a few decades later, scientists were on the verge of completing a massive project aimed at mapping the entire human gene complement.

Developments in genetic research and application as they affect humans, animals, and agriculture are the areas that have immediate ethical implications. We are going to examine some of the developments and their bioethical significance. Because of the almost inexhaustible body of literature, we will be able to do no more than examine representative topics and issues.

The Code of Life

Before we proceed to examine the various dimensions of genetic research and genetic therapy, we need to put some definitions in place.

First, the human body contains 100 trillion *cells*, the basic units of which all living things are made. Cells are the smallest units that retain the primary properties of life. Each cell contains DNA, the basic hereditary unit of life. The DNA is enclosed in a special compartment of the cell called the *nucleus*. The full complement of DNA in any organism is referred to as the *genome* of that organism.

The genome is divided into distinct segments called *chromosomes*. A chromosome is the microscopic, threadlike part of the cell that carries hereditary information in the form of *genes*. The human genome comprises 23 pairs of *autosomes* numbered 1 to 23 and one pair of sex chromosomes that are either XX for females or XY for males. A sex chromosome determines whether an individual is male or female.

Now, if we were to unravel a *chromosome*, we would get the long, threadlike *molecule* called DNA. DNA codes the genetic information needed for transmitting inherited traits. In all organisms DNA exists as a double-stranded molecule made up of four repetitive molecules called *bases*. A molecule is the smallest identifiable unit into which a pure substance can be divided and still keep its composition and chemical properties. The DNA bases are represented by the first letters of the molecules from which the DNA is made up: **A**=adenine; **T**=thymine; **C**=cytosine; **G**=guanine. The complexity of an organism's genome is directly proportional to the organism's complexity, from bacteria all the way up to humans. Imagine an alphabet that has only four letters. And imagine writing the entire genetic language through combinations of these four letters. That is precisely what God did.

Most of us need picture language to understand the DNA molecule. First, think of a twisted spiral staircase or ladder on which are rails on both sides (each a DNA strand). Each DNA strand is made up of molecules called *phosphate,* which are strung together to form the length of the strands (or ladder rungs). Each strand is called a *helix.* They are coiled together as the figure illustrates. The coiled double-stranded DNA molecule is therefore referred to as the *double helix.*

The steps of the ladder are made up of DNA bases that connect the two strands or rails. Each step is made up of two bases joined together by hydrogen bonds. The chemical structure of each base is such that an **A** must interact only with a **T** and with no other bases (A-T). The **G** will interact only with a **C** (G-C) and with no other base. Alterations in this arrangement (such as A-C, G-T) can alter the genetic code such that it transcribes and translates an altered protein, which has harmful effects in the organism.

In humans, the 23 pairs of *autosomes* and the pair of sex chromosomes contain all the bases of which there are approximately 3,000 megabases (1 million bases equals one megabase). Not all DNA on the chromosome is functional. Only 3 percent of the 3,000 human megabases encode information important for its function. Each chromosome then is made up of DNA, which is packaged into discrete functional genes and nonfunctional DNA between each gene, which is referred to as *intergenic* DNA.

The useful DNA on each chromosome is grouped together into discrete units called *genes*. Genes turn on and off to control our growth, body chemistry, and even the color of our hair and eyes. Some genes turn on early, some later. The number of DNA bases found in each gene varies from a few to several thousands of repetitive ATGC molecules. The order in which these bases appear constitutes the uniqueness of the gene and the gene product. The order of these DNA bases within each gene is referred to as the primary sequence of the gene. The major goal of the Human Genome Project is to determine the order of the genes on each chromosome, their sizes, and the primary sequence of each gene.

The predicted number of genes in the human genome ranges between 100,000 and 150,000 genes. The number may change when the entire genome is analyzed.

The structure of DNA has several important features. It provides the means for storing and coding vast amounts of information. The complementary structure allows for a faithful *replication* (reexpression, duplication) of DNA as cells divide. In replication the two strands unwind. Each acts as a template or pattern for new strands. A mechanism for preventing loss of genetic information is built into the DNA structure. A base that is lost or altered on one strand can be replaced by using the complementary strand to direct its repair. Amazingly, the complementarity of DNA permits strands to find each other in a complex mixture of molecules.

The Human Genome Project

The most astonishing development since 1953 has been the Human Genome Project, an international 13-year effort formally begun in October 1990. At a cost of over $3 billion, the project's overall goal is to decode the human gene. This includes efforts to (1) identify all the estimated 100,000-plus human genes and make them accessible for further study and (2) determine the complete sequence of the 3 billion DNA subunits (bases in the human genome). Sequencing is a prelude to figuring out what protein each gene produces and for what purpose.

The Department of Energy Human Genome Program and the National Human Genome Research Institute make up the United States Human Genome Project. The target date for completing the project is 2003. Using advanced computers to sequence genes, scientists expected to produce a "working draft" of the human genome in 2000.

Michael D. Lemonick and Dick Thompson describe the Human Genome Program in terms most of us can understand. It can be compared to "mapping out a route from San Francisco to New York City by walking the entire distance and noting every hill and valley along the way. It's slow but precise."[2]

On December 1, 1999, a team of more than 200 scientists from the United States, Japan, and England announced that they had crossed a major milestone in the Human Genome Project. They had completely sequenced chromosome number 22, the second smallest of the 23 pairs of human chromosomes. "The experience of being able to look at a chromosome in all of its detailed glory is hard to describe. It gives you chills; it gives you a sense of history," said Francis Collins of the National Institutes of Health. As it turns out, chromosome number 22 contains 545 genes, 298 of which were unknown to science until now. One malady directly related to defects in chromosome 22 is DiGeorge syndrome (more than 185 symptoms have been associated with the defect, including cleft palate, compromised immune systems, seizures, heart defects, facial deformities, and learning disabilities).[3]

Throughout most of the 10-year history of the Human Genome Project, the National Institutes of Health has been the recognized captain and leader of the project. But late into the project National Institutes of Health leadership was seriously challenged by an alternate effort. A bitter rivalry developed between scientists at the National Institutes of Health and Craig Venter and the company he founded—Celera Genomics. Both groups were rushing to map the human genome. Whereas the National Institutes of Health projected 2003 as its completion date (with a rough draft expected in 2000), Venter, a molecular geneticist, announced in 1999 that he would complete the task in 2001 or sooner. The official government project would spend $1.25 billion to complete its work. Celera Genomics would spend $330 million of private money to map the human genome, at one-third of the time and at no cost to taxpayers. Scientists interested in the Human Genome Project were split into two camps—one group siding with Venter and Celera Genomics, and the other group hoping that Venter would fail.

The second group will most likely be disappointed. In January 2000, Venter said he had completed a rough draft of the genome, months ahead of schedule. He announced that his company was on track to complete the project as early as the summer of 2000.[4] Then on April 6, 2000, Venter and Celera Genomics announced, "We've now completed the gene sequence of one human being." The person was an unidentified male. Venter added that by the end of that week Celera would have completed the gene sequence for a female. Venter restated his boast that Celera was far ahead of the government-funded Human Genome Project.[5]

Having the complete genetic blueprint for humans will transform medicine. The information will lead to new classes of drugs and to new kinds of treatments. The knowledge will help us understand diseases not by analyzing symptoms as has been largely true in the past, but by analyzing and understanding the genetic defects that produce them. Doctors may someday be able to diagnose diseases in persons long before they occur. And they will be able to prescribe medications that are custom-made to fit a patient's genetic profile.

Some of the realistic expectations are as follows. Scientists will soon have developed tests for assessing one's risks of cancer, diabetes, and stroke. They will have developed effective gene therapies for hemophilia, heart disease, and some forms of cancer. Sometime before 2015, scientists will have developed DNA tests that can analyze one's personal genetic makeup. By 2015 it is likely that medicine tailored to an individual's individual genetic composition will be available to treat diseases, including cancer. And by 2025, physicians are expected to be able to correct defective genes, thus making illnesses like sickle-cell anemia a thing of the past.

Two terms have entered our vocabulary: *genetic engineering* and *gene therapy.* Genetic engineering refers to actually altering genetic structure so as to prevent unwanted genetic expressions from occurring. Gene therapy refers to the use of genetic information in ways that treat and perhaps correct existing single-gene disorders. Gene therapy uses recombinant DNA technology to isolate and recombine a human gene that has therapeutic potential with the DNA from bacteria, yeast, or animal cell lines.[6] For example, genetic engineering technology is currently being developed for delivering the insulin gene back into a person with diabetes. This will be a more efficient and cost-effective form of treatment. However, the current gene delivery system needs more careful development.

Should Scientists and Companies Be Permitted to "Patent" Genetic Information?

In the public arena, particularly in the media, considerable controversy has erupted over whether scientists and companies should be permitted to "patent" genetic information. Though the controversy has substance, it often reveals a less-than-accurate understanding of the topic.

Joyce Tombran-Tink, a molecular biologist and researcher at the Stowers Institute for Medical Research in Kansas City, has sorted out the problem. She explains that when a gene is sequenced, a scientist can then understand the precise organization unique to each gene. Information about a gene's structure also provides the researcher with useful information about the protein the gene will encode and the protein's possible function in the organism. The gene can then be synthesized in a laboratory. The synthesized gene can subsequently be subcloned and efficiently translated into large amounts of the protein. The protein can then be used therapeutically in persons deficient in the gene in question or in persons who have a defective gene. So the therapeutic value of a gene lies in the expression of the protein it encodes. This, not the basic genetic information, is patentable. Tombran-Tink writes,

Being an inventor myself, patenting a gene is a very tedious process. There are many stringent guidelines associated with filing a patent application and its subsequent issuance. The furor surrounding the patenting of human genes weakens when one becomes aware of what is actually being patented. For example, the letters of the alphabet cannot be patented or its use restricted. The function of the alphabet is enormous. The letters can be used to write "God in the laboratory" which will then be copyrighted since it is the intellectual property of the author. The alphabet could also be used to write pornographic materials, the use of which should be restricted. However, the use of the alphabet should not be restricted because of some individuals who choose to use it to promote objectionable materials. Our personal autonomy and religious convictions allows us to make those choices regarding the kinds of literature we read and this has tremendous social impact. The alphabet serves no purpose unless it is used in creative and extraordinary ways to promote an idea. The idea then becomes copyright material. Similarly, once a gene sequence is known, the actual human gene is no longer needed since it can be synthesized in a laboratory and subcloned into a vector for gene therapy and other forms of genetic engineering methodologies.

The possible outcome of manipulating a gene sequence is enormous, and therefore, because it constitutes intellectual property rights, it becomes patentable. I would have to disagree with many bioethicists that patenting human genetic information for its potential use is analogous to patenting humans or "owning" human genes. While the genetic code is not the alphabet, an orderly alignment of the code is nonfunctional in itself unless it translates to a functional product. It is the effort placed into translating it and the potential outcomes that are the intellectual properties of the scientist. . . .

The human gene for insulin is a classic example of the therapeutic value of a gene product that has been employed in the genetic engineering technology. It would have been very sad for the human race if this gene had remained uncoded, unpatented, and unused.[7]

Given Tombran-Tink's helpful delineations, it is true that biotechnology and pharmaceutical companies are competing fiercely to capitalize on the fruits of genetic research. For example, in anticipation of big profits, by early 2000 investors had caused stock in Celera Genomics, the company inspired by Craig Venter, to advance handsomely.

Should private companies reap profits from research and development associated with the human genome? While some believe the answer should be no, Ted Peters disagrees. In May 1995, 180 religious leaders representing 80 different faiths and denominations signed "A Joint Appeal Against Human and Animal Patenting." The signers said, "We believe that humans and animals are creations of God . . . and as such should not be patented as human inventions."[8]

Peters asked, what did the signers have in mind regarding genetically engineered (transgenic) animals bred for medical purposes? These are life forms that did not previously exist. Are these animals, the result of human intervention, God's creations? Should the pharmaceutical companies that use transgenic animals in private research not be allowed to patent them? Research performed on transgenic animals might lead to medicines that the companies will also patent. "The loss of an exclusive market for a new drug, which a patent provides, would be a strong disincentive to rally the financial support to pursue research, and hence to find cures for diseases."[9]

Peters thinks that we should not sharply separate what God creates and what humans create. Since divine creativity is still going on, as scientists act creatively, "divine creativity and human creativity enjoy some overlap."[10]

Pluripotent Stem Cells: the "Biological Mother Lode"

In 1998 a breakthrough in genetic research occurred that is so potentially important that *Time* referred to it as striking the "biological mother lode." Scientists at the University of Wisconsin and another group at Johns Hopkins University isolated and successfully cultured human pluripotent stem cells. Stem cells have an unlimited capacity to divide and an ability to turn into most of the cells of the body. The scientists grew the cells for extended periods of time in culture dishes. The Johns Hopkins Medical Institutions Office of Communications and Public Affairs described the discovery as "one of basic science's holy grails."[11]

The "undifferentiated" cells have the capacity to grow into any sort of tissue the body will need—muscle cells, nerves, blood, heart, bone, and the rest. The cells came from fetuses aborted early in pregnancy. In an embryo, after a day or two at the most, the stem cells begin to differentiate. That is, they start the process of "specializing." As Michael Lemonick puts it, the cells "abandon their unlimited promise in order to do something useful with their lives."[12]

Hopes are that scientists can learn the mechanisms for stimulating pluripotent stem cells to develop into specialized cells. Perhaps the cells could then be used as replacement cells and tissue to treat many diseases and conditions, including Parkinson's disease, spinal cord injury, stroke, burns, heart disease, diabetes, osteoarthritis, and rheumatoid arthritis. At least theoretically, stem cells could be injected to patch up heart muscle damaged by cardiovascular disease. They might even be turned into neurons to replace brain cells destroyed by Alzheimer's disease, to provide new pancreatic cells that would pump insulin into the bloodstream of diabetics.

Knowledge gained from pluripotent stem cell research can improve our understanding of the complex events that occur during normal human development. It can also help us understand what goes wrong to cause birth defects and cancer.

Pluripotent stem cell research can change the way researchers develop drugs and test them for safety. Rather than going through the process of using animals for testing, drugs could initially be tested against a human cell line. Only the safest drugs would likely graduate to animal and then to human testing. The gain in efficiency and safety would be enormous.

But thoughtful critics have come forward to voice cautions that need to be observed. Biotechnology critic Jeremy Rifkin has urged the United States Congress to ban all privately funded research (he would include federally funded research) into embryonic stem cells. He thinks that there should first be a full investigation of the profound long-term social and ethical implications.

Persons opposed to induced abortions have also voiced objections. The stem cells with which the researchers work are taken from potential human beings, said Judie Brown, president of the American Life League: "These human beings should be protected by law." We should note that the sources of stem cells for the Hopkins researchers are fetuses aborted early in pregnancy. The Wisconsin group used blastocysts (clusters of about 140 cells that develop within a week after fertilization) left over from in vitro fertilization.[13]

Cloning

On February 23, 1997, the world awoke to learn a new name and to hear an amazing story: Dolly, a cloned sheep. For the first time of record scientists successfully cloned an adult mammal using DNA from a six-year-old sheep to create a genetically identical lamb—Dolly. The achievement was thought to be impossible by many experts. The scientists used the type of cloning that had been a subject of science fiction for years. The astonishing event and the clear technology that lay behind it immediately gave rise to the possibility of using the technology to clone humans.[14]

More immediately, the technology used to produce Dolly could make it possible to create clones of animals for biomedical research. The procedure may also be used to produce clones of commercial farm animals, such as dairy cows that give a large yield of milk. Cloning will provide insight into how DNA performs during fertilization, embryonic development, and old age. It will enhance the understanding of how human diseases develop and how to make better drugs to treat them.

In early March 2000, cloning technology took another step forward. An international biotechnology company announced that it had created a litter of genetically identical pigs. The company said that its eventual goal for pigs like these is to use them as organ donors for ailing persons. Someday, researchers hope, cloned pigs, whose organs are roughly the same size as those of humans, will be turned into tissue factories for human use.[15]

The appearance of Dolly unleashed a worldwide debate over the possibility of cloning humans. President Clinton ordered an advisory commission to study the moral implications of cloning. Rabbi Elliot Dorff has identified some of the most important ethical issues: First, who would be cloned? Second, how would the results of cloning be evaluated and by whom? Third, how would bad results be disposed of? Last, to what uses would cloning be put?

To the rabbi's questions others can be added. Perhaps the most fundamental question is "Does human cloning cross a moral and religious boundary that technology should never breech?" Would not human cloning represent the ultimate in human arrogance and self-worship?[16]

Gene Therapy

The headlines read "Gene Therapy Saves Two Babies."[17] On April 27, 2000, doctors in Washington, D.C., reported that two infants born with a life-threatening immune system disorder were living normal lives almost a year after undergoing an experimental genetic therapy. The two disorders had forced the two children to live inside protective "bubbles." If the children retain their good health, they will be the first in medical history to be

cured of a disease through gene therapy. Michael Blaise,
head of the human therapeutics division at Vali-Gen in
Newton, Pennsylvania, said, "This would probably be the
first example in any disease where gene therapy could be
a fully successful treatment."[18]

Perhaps the most astonishing, promising, and yet
morally problematic topic in genetic research and application is gene therapy (also called germ-line therapy). Gene
therapy offers a new way for curing human disease. Instead of treating the disease or symptoms of the disease
by using traditional medicines, the idea is to modify specific defective genes. Theoretically the result will be to cure
the disease by correcting the source of the problem. At
first gene therapy was envisioned for treating genetic disorders. Now, in addition, hopes are that gene therapy will
be effective in treating a wide range of diseases, including
cancer, arthritis, neurodegenerative diseases, and other acquired diseases. About 3,000 genetic disorders that can affect our health or well-being have been identified.

Gene therapy means the transfer of selected genes
into a host with the hope of moderating or even curing a
disease. Gene therapy seeks to rewrite bits of genetic
code in a patient's cells. Hardly a week goes by without
the press reporting news from the gene therapy front of
preliminary research results that yield hopes of treating
another disease through gene therapy.

A number of terms and concepts normally appear
alongside a discussion of gene therapy: (1) cell therapy
(genome therapy), which is the transfer of entire cells into
a host (the hope is that the transferred cells, which have
not themselves been genetically modified, will engraft into and improve the function of the host); (2) somatic gene
transfer, which is the transfer of genes to nongermline
tissues in the hope of correcting a disease; (3) germline
gene therapy, which is the transfer of genes to germline
(eggs or sperm) tissues in hopes of altering the cell complement (genome) of future generations.[19]

Some of the Moral Questions
That Genetic Research and Application Raise

The amazement we sense upon learning of developments in genetic research and its potential application is understandable. But the enormous array of ethical, legal, and social issues that the new developments in genetics have spawned leave us no less challenged. Persons in many sectors of public and private life—including frontline scientists—are exploring the moral implications and questions. They are looking for ways to make the coming new world of genetic research and application morally, socially, and legally responsible. By far, most of the persons involved at any significant level desire wisdom for governing research and application. But there is still a danger that noble goals will be subverted by persons and corporations driven more by ego and profit than by moral and social responsibility. We must never underestimate the subversive power of greed and ambition. Failure as a society to be vigilant will certainly lead to tragedy.

Let us now examine some of the moral issues the new world of genetic research and application generates. No order of importance is intended.

First comes a question that we might easily overlook. The goal of gene therapy is to correct a disability or a disorder. But setting the goal assumes that we know what a disability or disorder is. In many cases this is true. But in a project that can affect society on the scale that genetic engineering and gene therapy might, we must not assume that what is popularly perceived to be a disorder or disability is in fact so. We need to be aware that judgments about what constitutes a disorder may not be decided by purely objective criteria. Sometimes social prejudices and preferences also enter as unrecognized criteria. So we must remain vigilant against prejudices that in the name of objectivity would simply jeopardize those among us who are vulnerable. There is a possibility that behind our definition of "normal" lurks the tyranny of "the desirable society." For the Nazis numerous sorts of persons were judged to possess "disorders" that left them outside social protection. "Disorders" must not exploit those among us who cannot speak for themselves or who cannot bend political power in their favor.

A second moral question is "Do the targeted diseases really need to be cured or prevented?" What is the most effective and equitable way to invest limited monetary, medical, and personnel resources in preventive or curative medicine? The latter is more immediate but limited in its impact. The former does not have an immediate "payoff," but it does stand to have much broader and long-lasting ameliorative results.

Third is the danger that attention will be directed to "glamour" diseases rather than to those where research can make the broadest possible impact. Now we are back to the problem of a just allocation of limited resources. In this case, it is unjust to allow the "squeaky wheel" to receive the oil.

A fourth moral concern revolves around the profit interests of biotechnology firms. Without discounting the beneficial intentions of the biotechnology firms, the bottom line is that as publicly held companies, they are in business to make a profit. Their shareholders demand this. This is not necessarily wrong. But what happens when we mix the interests of scientific research with the driving forces of Wall Street? Traditionally, scientists in university labs have been free to practice good science that is not immediately aimed at products and profit. The developing story surrounding the Jesse Gelsinger case highlights this danger.

What will happen when the career and monetary interests of some gene therapists promote extravagant, or at least overly optimistic, public statements about contemporary gene therapy? How will these interests affect one's choices of research subjects? Are we facing a situation in which the disorders that "need" to be cured will be largely determined by who has the money to fund the research? Clearly, to the extent that this were to happen, research would have lost any claim to moral responsibility. Science would have been forced to serve in a shop for which it was never intended.

Fifth, fairness in the use of genetic information by insurers, employers, courts, schools, adoption agencies, law enforcement personnel, and the military, among others, is a matter of immediate concern. Who should have access to a person's genetic information? And under what circumstances might the information be used in a morally and socially responsible manner? Does an employer, for instance, who is about to invest corporate resources in an employee, have a right to access the candidate's genetic information?

With genetic information in hand, will employers be motivated to hire employees whose genetic screens show that they have a low likelihood of being subject to illness? Will genetic information create a new employee caste system? And what kind of governmental controls will be necessary to guard against abuse? "Ultimately, pre-employment genetic screening will effectively eliminate some people from the job market altogether."[20]

A sixth moral concern that has to be taken seriously is the possible psychological and social stigmatization that might increasingly occur in the future due to an individual's genetic differences. While serious observers are not predicting the arrival of "Gattaca," no one should ignore the impact that "social undesirability" can have on persons and even on whole groups of persons. The 20th century left a sorry record of "undesirability."

We must also be alert to the subtle if not overt pressures that might be brought to bear on persons, or whole groups of persons, who do not take advantage of the "genetic opportunities" science will offer.

Many people realize that we are swimming in dangerous waters. Daniel Callahan, a leading bioethicist, is alert to the danger of a "fascism" of health and genetic correctness. He means by this a social imposition of criteria for "normalcy" that either subtly or overtly coerce them to accept standards they might not want. New medical technologies, Callahan notes, "rarely remain discretionary for long. If they are not legally imposed on people . . . they can just as effectively be imposed by social pressure."[21]

Assisted reproductive technologies and protection of genetic information point up a seventh cause for moral vigilance. By what criteria can we reasonably insure that health-care professionals will use genetic information in ways that are morally responsible? Use of such information must show full respect for the dignity and moral values of the prospective parents and the value of the prospective child. By what standards can we insure that health-care personnel will properly counsel parents about the risks and limitations of genetic technology?[22]

Joyce Tombran-Tink calls our attention to an eighth factor that has both technical and moral importance. She speaks of the danger of accidentally eliminating species barriers that are needed to maintain our distinctives as humans. Species barriers could be breached through "horizontal gene transfer."[23]

Finally, it is becoming increasingly clear to many that technologies permitting genetic research and application are extremely expensive. They are likely to be supportable largely by private industry only. Who should and who will have access to the benefits biotechnology produces? Will rich and famous persons, or the rich nations alone, be the ones to reap the benefits while seated at the top of the medical technology hierarchy?

Who will pay for the use of these technologies? Should governments use taxation and wealth distribution to guarantee a reasonably equitable access to biotechnology? Or should we just admit that with wealth goes privilege, with poverty goes certain deficits? That's just the way the world is stacked.

9

REPRODUCTIVE
TECHNOLOGIES

Throughout the fall of 1997, much of the world waited for news from Iowa. Then on November 19, at the Methodist Medical Center in Des Moines, a 29-year-old Iowa seamstress, Bobbi McCaughey, gave birth to four boys and three girls in six minutes. Delivered by Caesarian section, the babies weighed a combined 18 pounds and 10 ounces. Forty specialists attended Bobbi. A devout Christian, she called the births a miracle. "God gave us those kids—He wants us to raise them," she said. On a more mundane level, the births were one more example of how "successful" the relatively new fertility drugs such as perganol can be. The seven children are the world's only surviving set of septuplets.

"I would consider this a miracle," said Paula Mahone, one of two lead physicians. "As we delivered each baby and saw the size of the babies and how vigorous they were, we were very, very happy."

McCaughey was almost three weeks beyond the point at which her physicians considered the fetuses viable. "It's absolutely incredible medically that she went that long," says Norman Duerbeck, an obstetrics professor at Southern Illinois University School of Medicine.

The hospital bill alone for the births and care of the seven babies ranges between $325,000 and $647,000. The figure could reach $1.25 million. The McCaugheys had medical insurance, but at the time no one knew how much of the bill the plan would cover. Their church set up a fund to assist the family.[1]

When the septuplets reached age two, several of them had prematurity-related complications. Alexis, the smallest at birth, could not walk and had to be fed through a tube.[2] Natalie was also being tube-fed. Nathan had just taken his first steps with a walker. Alexis and Nathan were working with occupational and physical therapists twice weekly.

As this story illustrates, in recent years momentous powers over human reproduction have become available to parents. The demand for resources devoted to the treatment of infertility has exploded. New techniques for overcoming infertility (such as artificial insemination, microsurgery, fertility drugs, and in vitro fertilization) have become standard. The new technologies are generating changes in traditional ideas about procreation, biologic roots, parental responsibility, and the institution of the family.

The Problem

The American Society for Reproductive Medicine defines infertility as a disease of the reproductive system that impairs the ability to conceive. Approximately 15 to 20 percent of all married couples are infertile, which means that they have not been able to conceive, resulting in a live birth, after 6 to 12 months of regular sexual intercourse (with no form of birth control). There are numerous reasons for infertility, and more than one problem may be present in a couple.

Infertility affects 6.1 million American women and their partners, about 10 percent of the reproductive-age population. Infertility is a disease of the reproductive system that affects men or women with almost equal frequency. Recent improvements in medication, microsurgery, and in vitro fertilization techniques make pregnancy possible for more than half of the couples pursuing treatments. In some instances infertility can be resolved short of using assisted reproductive technology. Drugs are sometimes used to treat an underlying disease or infection or hormone deficiency. In other instances sperm washing may enhance the husband's sperm. This involves treating the husband's sperm to remove unhealthy sperm cells or other factors that cause the uterus to reject the sperm. In some instances in which the fallopian tubes are blocked, displaced, or scarred, micro-laser surgery may be used to correct the problem.[3]

More than 70,000 babies are born each year in the United States as a result of all assisted reproductive technologies, including 45,000 as a result of in vitro fertilization.

Artificial Insemination

Artificial insemination is the use of other than natural means to insert semen into a female to fertilize a female egg for the purpose of achieving pregnancy. In humans, artificial insemination is normally used to treat subfertile men who have fertile female partners. Couples with infertility due to a male problem, such as low seminal volume, low sperm concentration, or decreased semen mobility, may be candidates for the procedure. Artificial insemination may also be employed when certain problems exist in the woman that make natural fertilization impossible.[4] It is a relatively simple and painless procedure that is performed in a doctor's office without an anesthetic.

In one technique, called intrauterine insemination, the physician places sperm directly into the uterus near the time of ovulation. In some instances more than one insemination is performed to ensure that insemination occurs at ovulation.[5]

There are two forms of artificial insemination: artificial insemination by husband and artificial insemination by donor.

Artificial Insemination by Husband

The first form is used to achieve pregnancy when, because of some physical or psychological problem suffered by either the husband or the wife, conception cannot be achieved through normal sexual activity. It is often used in instances in which the sperm count of the husband is too low. The husband's semen may be collected to increase the sperm count, or it may be augmented by that of a donor to achieve greater efficacy. The risks associated with AIH are minimal if the procedure is carefully conducted.

Although artificial insemination by husband raises relatively few moral questions, some reservations have been expressed. First, some persons question the morality of the procedure when it is used to control sex selection of the fetus. Second, some persons object to what they see as a separation of procreation from sexual expression. The objection is that it makes reproduction excessively technological. The Roman Catholic Church gave qualified approval to the procedure in 1987, but only in those instances in which it is not a "substitute for the conjugal act, but serves to facilitate and to help so that the act attains its natural purpose. . . . If, on the other hand, the procedure were to replace the conjugal act, it is morally illicit."

Artificial Insemination by Donor

Artificial insemination by donor is used to treat the infertile couple when the sperm count of the husband is too low to fertilize the female egg and the wife is potentially fertile. There are numerous causes for male infertility. In addition to infertility, there are other situations in which this procedure may be used, such as when the husband has a known hereditary or genetic disorder.

In some instances, however, the procedure is used for the purpose of trying to produce offspring with super-intelligence. The Nobel prize winner's sperm bank in California has this as its purpose. In the United States and Western Europe there is an increasing use of this method by single women who wish to have children but who do not desire marriage. Estimates are that 1 out of 10 recipients of artificial insemination by donor is unmarried.[6] If procedures are followed according to prevailing professional standards, donors are carefully screened to match characteristics similar to those of the husband. Before insemination with donor sperm occurs, the sperm are carefully tested, frozen for at least six months, and then stored to enable screening and prevention of communicable diseases. Therapeutic insemination with donor sperm is used in cases of

- Male sterilization
- Ejaculation problems
- Poor sperm penetration
- Immunologic infertility (a disorder in the immune system)

Therapeutic insemination by donor sperm is confidential, and the husband has sole rights to fatherhood.

Moral Objections to Artificial Insemination by Donor

Most of the moral questions prompted by artificial insemination arise in relationship to artificial insemination by the exclusive use of a donor. This procedure involves a deliberate disjunction between social and biologic (sperm donor) fatherhood. The former is made possible without the latter. According to research, artificial insemination by donor is held to be morally objectionable by most of the world's religions.[7]

On a general level, some reasons for rejecting the use of this method have been set forth. First is concern that the procedure might create psychological problems in the husband and wife. Second, one must consider the risk of transmitting serious genetic disorders or infectious diseases by the use of donor sperm. Third is concern about the occurrence of consanguinity (blood relationship) through excessive use of the same donor. Fourth, parents must consider the effect it may have on the resultant child, as well as on the family relationship. The need to maintain secrecy about the child's conception may interfere with healthy communication within the family. Further, psychological damage may result if the child were to inadvertently learn that artificial insemination by donor was responsible for conception.

There are far more important Christian reasons for rejecting this procedure. The most important problem it raises for Christians revolves around the morality of bringing a third party into the exclusive union of marriage. Many Christian ethicists believe that it violates the marital covenant because it severs procreation and marriage.

German theologian and ethicist Helmut Thielicke argued against Christian use of artificial insemination by donor from this basis. The moral error associated with it is that "here a third person enters into the exclusive psychological relationship of the marriage."[8]

Christian ethicist Paul Ramsey ruled out this type of insemination as acceptable for Christians because it violates the meaning of marital love as established by God. Marital love should reflect the love of God who bound himself to the world and the world to himself. In marital love a husband and wife similarly bind themselves to each other. God bound the nurturing of marital love and procreation together in the nature of human sexuality. "To put radically asunder what God joined together in parenthood when He made love procreative, to procreate from beyond the sphere of love, or to posit acts of sexual love beyond the sphere of responsible procreation (by definition, marriage), means a refusal of the image of God's creation in our own." Ramsey's reason as to why Christians should not engage in artificial insemination by donor is just as applicable today as it was in 1978: "Procreation and the communications of bodily love, nurturing and strengthening the bonds of life with life, belong . . .

together—not, it is true, in every act of marriage—but between two persons who are married."[9]

Edward D. Schneider adds another reason for judging artificial insemination by donor unacceptable for Christians: the moral assessment of the role played by the semen donor. "The donor exercises his procreative powers apart from any marital bond or commitment. He remains anonymously hidden from both the mother and the child, refusing his responsibility as father." Acting as nothing more than a sperm salesman, the donor fails "to take full responsibility for his biological offspring." His action is morally wrong because it "violates the fundamental unity of the personal and biological dimensions of sexual intercourse within the covenant of marriage."[10]

Some persons ask if artificial insemination by donor constitutes adultery. The answer depends on how one defines adultery. If adultery means a physical union outside of marriage, then it is not adultery. But if it includes conceiving a child by the semen of a man other than one's husband, then it would be an act of adultery.

Helmut Thielicke dismissed the notion that the use of artificial insemination by donor constitutes adultery. "One cannot call it adultery. Adultery requires a personal act of infidelity."[11]

Often, even Christians who agree with Thielicke and Ramsey say that adoption is a more acceptable option, because then the basic equality of the husband and wife is safeguarded.

Christian couples should carefully examine whether this practice violates the covenant of monogamy they made with each other. Does it unjustifiably introduce a third party into the commitment to mutual fidelity for better or for worse made by the husband and wife? And does it harmfully highlight the ability of one covenantal partner and the deficiency of the other? Does it indicate less than an "unreserved commitment to share another's life 'for better or worse, in sickness or in health'?"[12]

Surrogate Motherhood

Late in 1999, Arlette Schweitzer, a cheerful 42-year-old librarian from Aberdeen, South Dakota, was pregnant. But hers was a rather unusual pregnancy. She was serving as a surrogate mother for Christa, her daughter, and Kevin, her son-in-law. Christa had been born without a uterus. In February 1999, at the University of Minnesota Hospital and Clinic in Minneapolis, eggs harvested from Christa's ovaries were fertilized with Kevin's sperm. Then the embryo was transferred to Arlette's uterus. Ten days later Arlette telephoned Christa and Kevin. She exclaimed, "Congratulations! You're pregnant." Ultrasound later revealed that Arlette was carrying twins. At full term, Arlette—a devout Roman Catholic—gave birth to the children of Christa and Kevin—and to her own grandchildren.

Arlette had served as a surrogate mother. Surrogate motherhood is the bearing of a child by one person for another person. In the latter part of the 20th century, surrogate motherhood became an attractive option for many couples unable to give birth to their own children. Couples who choose surrogacy for reproduction want to have children who are their genetic offspring. So they choose to have another woman carry and give birth to their child. A quick survey of the Internet will show conversations between persons seeking the services of surrogate mothers and women interested in such a contract.

Surrogacy is often socially, legally, and morally complex. Laws in the United States that govern surrogacy vary widely. In 1997, Florida, Kentucky, Tennessee, Arkansas, Ohio, Nevada, and New Hampshire recognized surrogate motherhood as legal. Washington, Michigan, New York, Maryland, New Mexico, Utah, and Arizona had laws that criminalize surrogacy for pay. Twenty-four states had no laws regulating surrogate motherhood.[13]

Why would surrogate motherhood be used as a

means for childbirth? The option is employed when a woman is unable to provide either the genetic or the gestational components for childbearing. This may be because (1) she lacks a uterus, (2) pregnancy would be medically risky, (3) premature menopause has occurred, or (4) there is a risk of transferring a genetic defect to a child. One factor that has made surrogacy attractive is a decrease in the number of newborn white babies available for adoption.

Types of Surrogate Motherhood

There are two types of surrogate motherhood: gestational and genetic.

A surrogate *gestational* mother makes up for a deficit in function. Both the sperm of the intended father and the eggs of the intended mother are united, usually through in vitro fertilization, or the woman may be artificially inseminated. If in vitro fertilization is used, the resulting embryo is then placed in the surrogate mother. If pregnancy occurs, the surrogate will then provide the gestational component for reproduction and nothing else. She has no genetic link to the child. The woman who provides the egg will be the genetic mother.

Genetic surrogacy is different. A genetic surrogate mother makes up for a deficit in function and also in gamete. She provides the egg as well as the womb—so she is also the biological mother. Her eggs are inseminated (usually artificially) with the sperm of the intended father. This type of surrogate motherhood was at the center of the New Jersey court battle for custody of Baby M in 1987. According to the contract into which the parties enter, the surrogate mother will carry the pregnancy to full term and then willingly surrender the child to the custody of the genetic father and the adoptive mother. Prior agreements must be made regarding testing by amniocentesis and the possibility of an abortion if the fetus has genetic defects. If the child is born with genetic defects, the responsibility and care for the child rest squarely on the parents, not on the surrogate. "Surrogate . . . arrangements are designed to separate in the mind of the surrogate mother the decision to create a child from the decision to have and raise that child."[14] If it is discovered that the child is genetically the child of both the genetic surrogate and the husband of the surrogate, then the surrogate has responsibility for the child, unless adoption can be agreed upon.

Questions Regarding Costs and Legality

The costs associated with surrogate motherhood vary widely, depending on state laws and on which of the two types of surrogacy is used. The intended parents bear all costs.

In states where it is legal to do so, a surrogate mother can receive an agreed-upon fee for her services. In states where receiving a fee is considered criminal, the surrogate can be reimbursed for any medical, psychological, and living expenses directly linked to surrogacy. The same applies to prenatal care, maternity clothes, transportation, and possibly lost wages.

In some instances, women serve as surrogate mothers for an infertile friend or relative and charge no fee. But in most instances the surrogate mother is a stranger who receives compensation (which can vary in kind and amount) for her services. Paid surrogates average 25 years of age. More than one-half are married, one-fifth are divorced, and about one-fourth are single.

Moral Questions and Objections

Numerous objections have been lodged against both forms of surrogacy. Most of the objections are as applicable to one form as to another. But there is good reason to believe that a moral distinction should be made between gestational and genetic surrogacy. In genetic surrogacy a third person enters the marital covenant in a way that is not true of gestational surrogacy. The objections leveled earlier against artificial insemination by donor also apply with equal force to genetic surrogacy. But the objections do not apply equally to gestational surrogacy. One would be hard put to show how the marital covenant between Christa and Kevin was breached. From all appearances, the family engaged in a loving and supportive act. Such instances may be rare, but their dignity must not be overlooked in the debate regarding surrogacy. As we look at the standard objections, we should keep in mind the distinction between the two forms of surrogate motherhood.

The most often stated objection is that surrogacy is nothing more than child selling. This was the judgment of the New Jersey Supreme Court in the 1987 Baby M case. Even where the surrogate mother does not receive a fee, opponents say that it is wrong to give away a baby. But in the case of Arlette Schweitzer nothing resembling "selling" occurred.

It could be argued that in gestational surrogacy the baby does not belong to the mother in the same way that it does in genetic surrogacy. Proponents of surrogate motherhood counter that surrogacy should not be confused with baby selling because the fee paid is for a woman's services and not for the child itself.

The thinking behind the first objection is that the motive is wrong. For childbearing to be morally responsible the one who gives birth to the child must want it. If a woman acts responsibly, she will not become a surrogate. This argument can be challenged.

Surrogacy is morally suspect to some because it involves a change in motive for having children. The alleged change is "from a desire to have them for their own sake, to a desire to have them because they can provide some other benefit . . . to abdicate parental responsibilities."[15]

Opponents of surrogate motherhood ask, "Can we even begin to imagine the pain the child will feel in the future, torn between two families?" Furthermore, "What if the surrogate transfers serious genetic defects to the child?" Additionally, what about the psychological harm that might come to the surrogate mother when she returns the baby to the parents?

There is also a fear that participation by a surrogate mother in childbearing will weaken the marital bond and undermine the integrity of the family. Those who raise this concern believe that third-party involvement in procreation violates the marital covenant and threatens the sanctity of marriage.

Finally, there is a fear that surrogacy will lead to exploitation of poor and minority women by the well off.

Qualified Approval for Surrogacy in Some Instances

After a sober evaluation of surrogate motherhood, the Ethics Committee of the American Fertility Society expressed major reservations about surrogate motherhood but then stated limited conditions under which surrogacy might be morally defensible. The committee's statement is worth hearing.

> The committee does not recommend widespread clinical application of surrogate motherhood at this time. Because of the legal risks, ethical concerns, and potential physical and psychological effects of surrogate motherhood, it would seem to be more problematic than most of the other reproductive technologies. . . . The committee believes that there are not adequate reasons to recommend legal prohibition of surrogate motherhood, but it has serious ethical reservations about surrogacy that cannot be fully resolved until appropriate data are available for assessment of the risks and possible benefits of this alternative.[16]

The committee further recommended that surrogate motherhood should not be adopted for widespread use. The risk/benefit ratio of surrogacy does not justify it. The committee stressed the danger of abuse in the form of exploitation (such as financial enticement) and psychological intimidation by family members or others. The report compared payment for surrogacy to the sale of livers or kidneys, which is generally condemned.

But there have been instances of surrogate motherhood in which these fears did not materialize. In one such instance, a well-educated, highly articulate, upper-middle-class mother of three healthy children spoke to a group of seminarians about her desire to help a childless couple share the joy of childbirth and her resultant experience of surrogacy. She did not profit monetarily. Would she do it again? "Yes," she answered, "but only for the same family." No one listening to her could have properly concluded that she had been exploited or that she believed she had performed anything other than a loving and beautiful act.

Assisted Reproductive Technology

Due to astonishing developments in biotechnology, today there exists a wide array of procedures designed to unite sperm and eggs. These procedures completely bypass some of the factors that cause infertility. Collectively, they are called assisted reproductive technologies. Assisted reproductive technology usually involves the use of drugs (such as perganol) to stimulate the growth of as many eggs (oocytes) as possible. This increases the chances for fertilization and subsequently pregnancy.

We will examine some of the most often used forms of assisted reproductive technologies. They include: (1) in vitro fertilization, (2) gamete intrafallopian transfer, (3) zygote intrafallopian transfer. We will mention a couple of other procedures used in rare instances. Then we will briefly note a significant new development in assisted reproductive technology called "blastocyst transfer." We will also look at an even newer technique now being discussed but not yet developed, "embryo splitting."

In Vitro Fertilization Preembryo Transfer

On July 26, 1978, a remarkable baby, Louise Brown, was born in England. She was hailed as "the first test-tube baby of the world." The procedure that led to Louise Brown's birth was implemented by Drs. Robert G. Edwards and Patrick C. Steptoe. The phrase "test-tube baby" became fixed in popular parlance, but the phrase is incorrect. Louise Brown was conceived in vitro, that is, in a laboratory. *In vitro* is derived from Latin and means "in glass." So in vitro fertilization (in humans) refers to the fertilization of an egg outside the female body in an artificial environment, such as a glass container.

To achieve such a phenomenon, Drs. Edwards and Steptoe surgically removed an ovum from Louise's mother. They used an instrument called a laparoscope, which they guided through a small incision in the abdomen down to where the doctors could see the maturing ova. The laparoscope was then used to remove (harvest) an egg. The ovum was placed in a petri dish, where it was fertilized by the husband's semen. The fertilized ovum or embryo, after two and one-half days growth, was placed in the mother's uterus. It then implanted itself in the uterine wall and a normal pregnancy and childbirth resulted.

The Technical Aspects of In Vitro Fertilization. In vitro fertilization is a method of assisted reproduction in which a man's sperm and a woman's egg are combined in a laboratory. There fertilization occurs. The resulting embryo is then transferred to the uterus to develop naturally. Usually two to four embryos are transferred with each cycle. In vitro fertilization includes its more standard form and its variations. A new technique for recovering eggs from the ovary uses a sonographically guided needle that replaces the surgical procedure previously used to recover eggs. The more recent procedure is called transvaginal oocyte retrieval. It requires neither hospitalization nor general anesthesia.[17]

The possibility of a successful pregnancy being achieved for any one patient depends on many factors, including age and the reproductive health of both the wife and the husband. Since Drs. Edwards and Steptoe introduced the procedure, over 20,000 babies have been born worldwide by this method.

There are numerous reasons for the use of in vitro fertilization. First, the mother is fertile but unable to conceive. Second, the father is infertile, the mother is fertile but is unable to conceive. Third, the mother may be infertile (for example, her ovaries do not produce eggs) but she is able to carry a child. The father's sperm (or a donor's sperm) are used to fertilize a donor ovum, and the embryo is transferred to the womb of the mother who then gives birth to the child.[18] Fourth, the mother may be fertile but may still make use of in vitro fertilization because of increased maternal age, hormonal irregularities that impair normal egg production, or genetic problems that make the women's eggs unsuitable for assisted reproductive technologies. To increase the chances of success, donor egg in vitro fertilization is increasingly preferred for women over age 42. According to a 1999 *U.S. News & World Report* article, the use of donor eggs is soaring.[19] Fifth, both parents are infertile but the mother is able to carry a child. Sixth, the mother is unable to carry the child, but both parents are fertile. The solution is to extract ova from the mother, fertilize them with the sperm of the father, and then transfer the embryo to a surrogate who will give birth to the baby. Seventh, the mother is fertile but unable to carry the child; the father is infertile. So, the sperm of a donor are used to fertilize the ovum of the mother.

Arguments Against the Morality of In Vitro Fertilization. As may be expected, in vitro fertilization calls for careful moral consideration. There is no simple agreement among Christian ethicists regarding the procedure. Furthermore, some of the objections offered do not apply to all forms of this method.

The first objection is that in vitro fertilization separates procreation from sexual lovemaking. That is, it removes conception and parenting from its proper context. This objection assumes that for the good of the child, the couple, and society, conception should occur only where the natural conditions of procreation are observed. If standard in vitro fertilization, in which no third party is introduced is being considered, this objection taken by itself seems quite strained.

The second objection is that the procedure might result in the birth of a deformed or retarded child. In vitro fertilization exposes others to potential risks without their consent and is therefore an immoral means for achieving the birth of a child, opponents say.[20]

This objection has faults. The risks that a child born through this procedure will have birth defects are no higher than they are for a child born through natural conception. Second, parents can make the same commitment to love the child born through in vitro fertilization that any other parent can make.

A third objection is that in vitro fertilization uses expensive resources to produce more offspring in an already overpopulated world. It is immoral, the argument holds, to spend many thousands of dollars just for the experience of giving birth to one's own child, especially when adoption is less expensive and can provide a loving environment for a child deprived of a family.

The fourth objection is that ova successfully fertilized but not transferred to the mother are wasted. In vitro fertilization is morally wrong, opponents say, in part because the fetal waste it produces shows disregard for human life.

The fifth objection to the procedure is that it oversteps the limits of creaturely freedom. What we *can* do and what we *ought* to do are not always the same. Our enthusiasm for the new techniques that can overcome infertility, ethicist Arthur Caplan warns, "should not blind us to the fact that these techniques are still new, relative-

ly poorly understood, and surrounded with uncertainty as to their efficacy and safety."[21]
A sixth argument against in vitro fertilization has to do with its risks. Costs in time, money (clinic costs can range from $50,000 to $100,000), commitment, and emotional liability can leave a couple depleted even before a pregnancy occurs. And when in vitro fertilization results in multiple births, the risks (emotional, monetary, and so on) intensify. The most important objections to in vitro fertilization arise when a third party is introduced.

Arguments That Support the Morality of In Vitro Fertilization. When the arguments in favor of in vitro fertilization are compared with the arguments against it, one can easily see that Christians who are equally committed to Jesus Christ and to the ethic of the New Testament disagree sharply over whether or not in vitro fertilization is morally acceptable. Having fairly presented the arguments against this procedure, let's now do the same with the reasons given for *accepting* it.

First, the Bible teaches we are created in the image of God. This means in part that we have been given powers of creativity that can advance the welfare of humanity and thereby glorify God. Medicine does not violate natural processes; it cooperates with them and participates in divine creativity. In vitro fertilization is simply one example of how imagination and intelligence can be used to creatively improve life.[22]

Second, in vitro fertilization was developed to help couples in distress. It was not developed to violate the limits of creaturely freedom or to satisfy the idle curiosity of scientists. If one uses the "limits" argument against the procedure, then it should have been used against the first efforts to transplant hearts or kidneys.

Third, if would-be parents yearn for a child of their own, we cannot justifiably tell them that adoption is better than in vitro fertilization. Furthermore, adoption procedures are complex and lengthy, and success is not guaranteed.

Fourth, in vitro fertilization is a way of relieving the suffering of infertile couples. If doctors have the ability to relieve the anguish of an infertile couple—an anguish too deep to be appreciated by most persons who have no reproductive problems—then why should they not respond?[23]

The fifth argument in favor of this method is that benefits outweigh costs. Who is to say that the costs of in vitro fertilization cannot be justified? A couple can employ it to satisfy their deep parental and emotional needs. By giving birth to a child, they may in fact be using their resources generously rather than selfishly.

Gamete Intrafallopian Transfer

Gamete intrafallopian transfer was developed in 1984 by Dr. Ricardo H. Asch and his colleagues at the University of California, Irvine. As a procedure used to assist in achieving pregnancy, gamete intrafallopian transfer is even more recent than in vitro fertilization. When at least one fallopian tube is open, gamete intrafallopian transfer can be used as an alternative to in vitro fertilization. Gamete intrafallopian transfer occurs in the fallopian tube. A mixture of sperm and eggs[24] is placed directly into one of the woman's fallopian tubes (the normal site of fertilization) in a surgical procedure using either laparascopy or minilaparascopy. This duplicates the way a normally fertilized egg would begin its journey to the uterus for implantation.

Unlike standard in vitro fertilization, in which the question will likely arise, "What is to be done with the extra embryos?" in gamete intrafallopian transfer, embryos are created in the fallopian tubes. Either sperm and eggs come together naturally or no embryo results. If eggs are "wasted," this is nothing more than what naturally occurs in the menstrual cycle. For this reason, many persons who reject in vitro fertilization because they think that eliminating extra fertilized eggs is morally wrong find gamete intrafallopian transfer morally acceptable. In this method, if any fertilized eggs do not implant and mature, the failure is a natural one. The moral questions associated with gamete intrafallopian transfer occur at another level. With this procedure there is a good possibility that multiple conceptions and hence multiple births will occur. Early studies suggest that about 30 percent of all term pregnancies resulting from gamete intrafallopian transfer are twins. Before electing this procedure, couples must answer a critical question: Are we prepared to bring to term each embryo that results from this procedure, or will we abort if there are multiple conceptions?

The likelihood that twins would be born is relatively high. The likelihood that four or more conceptions will occur is quite low. But such results are definitely possible.

Intrauterine Insemination

Intrauterine insemination uses the sperm preparation techniques of in vitro fertilization, concentrates the best sperm, and then places them high in the uterus to increase the likelihood that fertilization will occur. The process is often combined with fertility drug stimulation. As is true for gamete intrafallopian transfer, fertilization occurs.

Zygote Intrafallopian Transfer

Zygote intrafallopian transfer combines aspects of both in vitro fertilization and intrauterine insemination. The procedure for ovarian stimulation is identical to those used for in vitro fertilization and gamete intrafallopian transfer. Like both, it takes advantage of the fallopian tube as nature's incubator. One difference between gamete intrafallopian transfer and zygote intrafallopian transfer is that in the zygote intrafallopian transfer procedure the ova are collected and are then fertilized in the laboratory. Unlike standard in vitro fertilization, the embryo is placed in the women's fallopian tube through the use of a laparoscopy rather than through the uterus. On average, the success rate of zygote intrafallopian (deliveries per retrieval) is 24.4 percent.

Blastocyst Transfer

Carolyn Bell knows that she has the strength for only one more round of fertility treatments. The pain involved in conceiving her first child—hormone shots twice a day, the medical complications that left her hospitalized, and the two miscarriages that occurred during her pregnancy with triplets—rested fresh on her mind.

Now the 37-year-old federal prosecutor is considering having a second child. She turns to a promising new development in reproductive technology: blastocyst transfer. A blastocyst is a highly developed embryo (usually developed by day five or six after fertilization) that has divided many times over to a point where it is composed of 100 or more cells. At this stage, it is nearly ready to implant on the walls of the uterus. A blastocyst has come a long way from its beginning as a single cell and is much more complex than it was even at day three (typically at the eight-cell stage).[25]

Blastocyst transfer is an advanced form of in vitro fertilization and is reducing the strain on women who face the desperation of not being able to give birth to a child naturally. The procedure is also reducing the consequences of costly multiple births from infertility treatments such as occurred in the case of Bobbi McCaughey. Blastocyst transfer is growing in popularity in the United States.

Embryo Splitting for Infertility Treatment

A technique for treating infertility currently being considered is "embryo splitting." Early embryonic cells are *totipotent* (capable of giving rise to all of the different cell and tissue types [such as liver, brain, and bone] required for making a complete and viable mammal).

Therefore, there is the possibility of splitting or separating early preimplantation embryos (before being implanted in the womb). The purpose would be to increase the number of embryos that can be used for in vitro fertilization. Embryo splitting would result in two or more embryos having identical genetic composition (that is, the same genome, one's complete complement of genes).

Splitting one embryo into two or more could help infertile couples in several ways. For couples who can produce only one or two embryos, splitting could increase the number of embryos available for transfer. Because the in vitro fertilization pregnancy rate increases with the number of embryos transferred, embryo splitting would enhance the likelihood that pregnancy will result. For couples who produce more than enough embryos for one cycle of transfer, splitting one or more embryos could provide sufficient embryos for subsequent transfers without having to go through another retrieval cycle. Whether the process is technically feasible for humans has yet to be demonstrated.

Already a number of ethical objections to embryo splitting have been raised. One objection is that embryos will be manipulated and some will be destroyed in the process of research and application. Another objection is that identical twins may be deliberately created, and then they might be born several years apart. Some observers have also noted that the technical ability to split embryos might lead couples to have embryos split, not for therapeutic reasons, but to provide "backup" embryos in case an existing child needs a tissue or organ transplant. Fears have also been voiced that embryo splitting could create a market for "stored" embryos whose genetic traits are desirable.

Those who believe that embryo splitting shows promise of delivering important therapeutic benefits believe that the technique could be exercised under moral

constraints. Supporters maintain that as long as couples
are fully informed, there should be no significant moral
objection to transferring two or more embryos with the
same genetic structure. The birth of identical twins already occurs naturally and on a regular basis.[26]

On January 14, 2000, the prospects of using embryo
splitting for treating human infertility took on a new ur-
gency. The journal *Science* reported experimental success
for embryo splitting. Oregon researchers reported the
birth of Tetra, a female rhesus monkey. Tetra resulted
from splitting an eight-cell embryo into four parts. Three
of the developing monkeys did not survive. Professor Gerald Schatten, a researcher at the Oregon Health Sciences
University in Portland, said four more genetically identical animals were on the way.[27]

CONCLUSION

Now that we have completed our survey of bioethics, we will conclude by providing guidance for making bioethical decisions. The counsel to be offered seems to assume that a person, a spouse, or a family will have plenty of time to reflect on and weigh options. In many instances this will be true. In many other situations decisions must be made on short notice. In such instances emotions may already be frayed, energies taxed, and mind and spirit weary. That is why all of us should have in place some values and steps that can be relied upon, and that can lead beyond the tendency to act impulsively. One thing we can do in advance is to write and properly record (and to urge competent family members to do the same) our health-care directives, advance directives, and durable power of attorney. Another is to sign and carry universal donor organ cards. Standardized forms are available.

First, the most important thing Christians need to remember when making bioethical decisions is that we are reconciled to God by grace through faith alone, not by works. This includes "not by perfect decisions in the crises of life." There exists a distorted legalistic form of Christianity that paralyzes people, making it impossible to act creatively and decisively. This is sometimes referred to as a performance-based Christianity. The idea is that God accepts us on the basis of how perfectly we "perform." The apostle Paul, Martin Luther, and John Wesley are just a few of the Christians who at one time lived under the tyranny of "performance." And they are just a few of those who came to see that "anyone who belongs to Christ is a new person. The past is forgotten, and everything is new. God has done it all!" (2 Cor. 5:17-18, CEV).

Knowing that we are graciously embraced by the Father through His Son should not invite carelessness and irresponsibility. But it does set us free to make difficult decisions, the outcomes of which we know will be less than perfect and probably displeasing to some. The grace of God sets us free to make difficult calls without landing us in a sea of guilt, despair, or endless second-guessing. Christians who know that the gracious Father embraces them in His Son and by the Holy Spirit can act with confidence even when they can't act ideally. We live by "gifts," not by achievements.

Second, the time to begin preparing to make bioethical decisions is when life is relatively peaceful and free of major crises. And though no one should ever boast that he or she "is ready for anything," we can diligently develop Christian virtues and Christian wisdom that will prepare us to make choices that rise above impulsiveness, panic, and helplessness. There is a world of difference between a Christian who diligently pursues the way of discipleship, learning the mind of Christ by dwelling in the great Christian story, and one who does not.

Christian wisdom and virtue come through the Holy Spirit. He teaches us through life in the Body of Christ and by practicing Christian virtues until they become who we are. And none of this will occur unless we dwell in the Scriptures until the Story of God—God with His people and with His world—comes to dwell in us. The person marked by Christian virtue is a "story-shaped" person.

In some instances, the Bible will clearly light the pathway to making bioethical decisions. In other instances it will not, and should not be expected to give explicit answers to complex biotechnical- and biomedical-related questions.

Churches should be communities of the Spirit that carefully explore how to embody and practice Christian convictions. Here we should prepare for effective witness in the world by becoming equipped to behave in ways, and make decisions, that are characteristically Christian. In the New Testament Church, no "lone rangers" were endorsed. No one was permitted to think that he or she could live in Christ, isolated from essential dependence on his or her sisters and brothers in the Lord. Nor should we.

Third, the next element in the process of making bioethical decisions is to gather pertinent information. As time and resources permit, pull together the data that bear directly on the question or crisis at hand. If necessary, insist on receiving all the information one needs in order to make intelligent and responsible decisions. Don't be intimidated by the sometimes-daunting edifice of modern medicine. Neither technology, complex hospitals, nor health-care professionals are more important than a person's or a family's right to make informed, owned decisions.

Be concerned not only with what you already know but also with what you need to know. Sometimes just having sufficient information in hand resolves a problem. Also, let us not hesitate to admit what we don't know. In most cases, professionals are willing to assist if we are willing to admit that we need help. One must be careful about using the Internet as a source of information. Almost anyone can place misleading information on the Web. So bring to the Web a healthy dose of skepticism.

Nevertheless, there are some good resources (all of which must be used with discretion) to which we can turn. There are some that stand at the head of the list as sources for medical information. The first one is provided by the National Institutes of Health, called Health Information, www.nih.gov/health. The second is www.healtfinder.gov, a consumer-friendly gateway to reliable medical sites both inside and outside the United States government. The third source is www.mayo.edu, home of the Health Oasis, which tackles questions ranging from cracked knuckles to Paget's disease. The fourth is www.medscape.com, a favorite of health-care profes-

sionals. It offers online classes for credit, summaries of research meetings, and much more.

Other excellent sources are the National Institutes of
Health Bioethics on the Web
(http://www.nih.gov/sigs/bioethics/index.html); NOAH:
New York Online Access to Health
(http://www.noah.cuny.edu/); The Figo Committee for
the Study of the Ethical Aspects of Human Reproduction
(http://www.md.huji.ac.il/figo/INDEX.HTM);
About.Comtm (http://genetics.about.com/education/ge-
netics/); and MedicineNet.com (http://www.medi-
cinenet.com/Script/Main/hp.asp).

Fourth, identify the ethical issues. One of the dangers we face when making bioethical decisions is to permit our biases and emotions to determine our assessment
of a problem and its options for solution. As dispassion-
ately as possible and by taking advantage of objective
counsel from informed friends or pastors, identify the ethical issues and options for action.

Fifth, which Christian convictions have a bearing on
the crisis at hand? In this particular situation, do some
Christian convictions weigh more heavily or are more applicable than others? Remember the balanced Christian
convictions we studied earlier: freedom and stewardship;
the sanctity and relative value of life; individuality and
social solidarity; and the Christian appraisal of technology.

Sixth, identify the alternative choices. Some alternatives can be ruled out quickly. But in many instances the
alternatives have both attractive and negative features.
Trying to weigh all of this for the good of someone else or
for oneself is what makes decisions difficult.

Of all the alternatives that have been identified,
which one will best embody the Christian convictions
that most urgently need to be observed here? Which alternative will show greatest fidelity to the vision of human life that the Christian Story sets forth? Which course

of action will most likely bring glory to God and show faithfulness to the gospel of Jesus Christ?

Seventh, choose in confidence, and trust in the God of sovereign grace. Remember—we are not saved by how perfectly we can gain God's perspective on the world but by radical trust in His faithfulness to His people. Remember that when one chooses in this way he or she does so in faith. The Spirit will give strength to act and the power to live in the comfort of God's grace.

Eighth, one of the most important things Christians should remember is that we neither live nor die as those "who have no hope." By how we live and die, we Christians should demonstrate to our families and friends our defining conviction that the value of biological life is transcended by eternal life—life in the crucified and resurrected Lord. We are not materialists. "Now you have eternal life," Jesus said. The apostle Paul spoke as a Christian, not as a pagan, when he wrote, "I consider that our present sufferings are not worth comparing with the glory that will be revealed to us. . . . No, in all these things we are more than conquerors through him who loved us. For I am convinced that neither death nor life, neither angels nor demons, neither the present nor the future, nor any powers, neither height nor depth, nor anything else in all creation, will be able to separate us from the love of God that is in Christ Jesus our Lord" (Rom. 8:18, 37-39). Can Christians currently live and die in this confidence? They can if the crucified Christ was raised on Easter. They can if Pentecost happened. They can if the Apostles' Creed is true.

NOTES

Introduction

1. J. Richard Middleton and Brian J. Walsh, *Truth Is Stranger than It Used to Be: Biblical Faith in a Postmodern World* (Downers Grove, Ill.: InterVarsity Press, 1995), 172-76.

2. Warren Thomas Reich, ed., *The Encyclopedia of Bioethics* (London: Simon and Schuster and Prentice-Hall International, 1995), 1:xxi.

3. Ibid.

4. Thomas A. Shannon, *An Introduction to Bioethics*, 3rd ed. (Mahwah, N.J.: Paulist Press, 1997), 4.

5. Tom L. Beauchamp and James F. Childress, *Principles of Biomedical Ethics*, 4th ed. (New York: Oxford University Press, 1994), 3.

6. Ibid.

7. John F. Kilner, Nigel M. de S. Cameron, and David L. Shiedermayer, *Bioethics and the Future of Medicine* (Grand Rapids: William B. Eerdmans Publishing Co., 1995), 147-48.

8. Reich, *Encyclopedia of Bioethics*, xix.

9. Jonathan D. Moreno, *Deciding Together: Bioethics and Moral Consensus* (New York: Oxford University Press, 1995), 88.

10. Gene chip technology is already being used by many pharmaceutical companies and small laboratories. With recent advances toward large-scale sequencing of the genome, thousands of human genes are embedded on postage-stamp-size glass chips. These microarray fabrications are fully automated for high throughput gene screen. The human gene chips currently available contain between 7,000 and 10,000 human genes, but this array will expand to include fragments of all human genes when the HOP is completed. These chips are currently being used to identify complex polygenic diseases, subtype diseases, drug discovery, toxicology, and pathogen analysis. The potential impact of microarray technology in preventive medicine is enormous. It promises more targeted drug treatment interventions where drugs are designed to treat the disease causes rather than the symptoms.

11. Justice Scalia, concurring in the majority opinion, *Cruzan v. Missouri Department of Health (1990),* Majority Opinion, written by Chief Justice William Rehnquist, *Today's Moral Issues: Classic and Contemporary Issues*, 3rd ed., ed. Daniel Bonevac (Mountain View, Calif.: Mayfield Publishing Co., 1999), 441.

12. See Thomas Berry and Brian Swimme, *The Universe Story* (San Francisco: HarperSanFrancisco, 1992).

13. For a discussion of the relationship between bioethics and the practice of medicine see Gilbert C. Meilander, *Body, Soul, and Bioethics* (Notre Dame, Ind.: University of Notre Dame Press, 1995), chap. 1.

14. Stanley Hauerwas, *A Community of Character: Toward a Constructive Social Ethic* (Notre Dame, Ind.: University of Notre Dame Press, 1981), 30-31.

15. James Gustafson, "Theology Confronts Technology and the Life Sciences," *On Moral Medicine: Theological Perspectives in Medical Ethics,* ed. Steven E. Lammers and Allen Verhey (Grand Rapids: William B. Eerdmans Publishing Co., 1987), 41.

Part 1

1. For an extended discussion of influential religious and secular approaches to bioethics, see Scott B. Rae and Paul M. Cox, *Bioethics: A Christian Approach in a Pluralistic Age* (Grand Rapids: William B. Eerdmans Publishing Company, 1999), 7-87.

Chapter 1

1. Richard B. Hays, *The Moral Vision of the New Testament* (San Francisco: HarperSanFrancisco, 1996), 196.

Chapter 2

1. Most of the material in this section is adapted from Al Truesdale, "Preface to Bioethics," *Perspectives on Science and Christian Faith: Journal of the American Scientific Affiliation* 48 (1996): 224-29. Used by permission.

2. James F. Childress, *Priorities in Biomedical Ethics* (Philadelphia: Westminster Press, 1981), 102.

3. Douglas John Hall, *The Steward: A Biblical Symbol Come of Age* (New York: Friendship Press, 1984).

4. Ibid., 24.

5. Hans Walter Wolff, *Anthropology of the Old Testament,* trans. Margaret Kohl (Philadelphia: Fortress Press, 1974), 3.

6. Ibid., 1-2.

7. Karl Barth, "Respect for Life," *Church Dogmatics,* trans. A. T. Mackey, et al. (Edinburgh: T. and T. Clark, 1961), 3:363.

8. Martin Luther King Jr., *Why We Can't Wait* (New York: Signet Books, 2000), 77.

9. Wolff, *Anthropology of the Old Testament,* 214.

10. Paul Ramsey, *Basic Christian Ethics* (New York: Scribners, 1950), 234-48, 388.

11. David Neff, "The Eugenic Temptation," *Christianity Today* 34 (19 November 1990): 23.

12. See Harman L. Smith and Paul Lewis, "A Protestant View of Reproductive Technologies," *Second Opinion* 14 (July 1990): 94-106.

13. Daniel Bell, as quoted by Shannon, *Introduction to Bioethics,* 13-14.

14. "Fetal-tissue Work to Be Investigated," *Kansas City Star,* 8 March 2000, sec. B1; "FBI Opens Fetal Tissue Probe," *Kansas City Star,* 11 March 2000, sec. B1.

15. Jack W. Moore, "Human In Vitro Fertilization: Can We Support It?" *Christian Century,* 22 April 1981, 442-46.

16. Greg Barret, "Templeton Winner Has Faith: To Err Is Human and Divine," *USA Today*, 23 March 2000, sec. 10D. In 2000 Dyson was the winner of the Templeton Prize for Progress in Religion.

Chapter 3

1. According to a report in the *New England Journal of Medicine* (July 1988), 31 percent of all "implanting" embryos miscarry naturally, often before the woman realizes she is pregnant. According to reliable estimates as many as 75 percent of all fertilized ova never yield a live baby.

2. See Richard B. Hays's critique of Christians who appeal to "freedom of choice" as a Christian defense for abortion in Hays, *Moral Vision of the New Testament*, 453-55.

3. Elinor Burkett, "In the Land of Conservative Women," *Atlantic Monthly*, September 1996, http://www.theatlantic.com/politics/abortion/abortion.htm.

4. The statistics are based on numbers and estimates provided by the Alan Guttmacher Institute; sources for statistics for 1973 through 1992: Stanley K. Henshaw et al., "Abortion Services in the United States, 1991 and 1992," *Family Planning Perspectives* 26, No. 3 (May-June 1994): 101.

5. *USA Today*, 7 January 2000, Nationline, http://www.usatoday.com/

6. About 11 percent of all women having abortions live in Africa, 58 percent in Asia, and 9 percent in Latin America and the Caribbean. The remainder live in Europe (17 percent) and elsewhere in the developed world (5 percent). For every 1,000 women of childbearing age, 35 are estimated to have an induced abortion each year. Overall, women in developed and developing regions have strikingly similar abortion levels—39 procedures per 1,000 women and 34 per 1,000, respectively.

7. Thirty-nine percent of the world's women live under restrictive abortion laws: 25 percent in parts of the world where abortion is permitted only to save a woman's life, or is prohibited altogether; 10 percent live where abortion is allowed only when it is necessary to protect a woman's physical health or her life. The Alan Guttmacher Institute, 1999, http://www.agi-usa.org/pubs/fb_0599.html.

8. Currently the FDA is considering approval of another drug, methotrexate, for use as an alternative to surgical abortion.

9. Even before RU-486 received conditional FDA approval, a group of "frustrated" activists and doctors found a way to make limited supplies of RU-486 available. They set up a secret lab to make the drug and gained FDA approval to use the drug in trials.

10. "Partial-Birth Abortion Borders on Medical Malpractice," an article prepared by the Missouri chapter of the Physicians Ad Hoc Coalition for Truth, *Kansas City Star*, 13 September 1999, sec. B4.

11. Quoted by Martha Bayles, "Feminism and Abortion," *Atlantic Monthly*, April 1990, http://www.theatlantic.com/politics/abortion/abortion.htm.

12. Hays, *Moral Vision of the New Testament*, 446, 448.

13. Ibid., 48.

14. Ibid., 450.

15. Ibid., 452-53.

16. Volunteer members form an extensive employment, medical, educational, counseling, and residential network. The network enables a mother to continue the life of her unborn child without sacrificing her own hopes and dreams. It offers guidance, counseling, nurturing homes, medical and financial assistance, educational and career programs, adoption counseling and services. The Nurturing Network's toll-free number: 1-800-TNN-4MOM (http://www.nurturingnetwork.org/). An alarming current development in the United States is "Dumpster babies," infants abandoned under circumstances that will either cause serious harm or even death to the infant. Thanks to a creative grassroots movement, centers are being established across the nation that will permit mothers of unwanted infants "safely" to abandon unwanted newborns. For the full story of this development see Timothy Roche, "A Refuge for Throwaways," *Time*, 21 February 2000, 50-51. A "Baby Bank" has been established in Hamburg, Germany, that serves the same purpose.

Chapter 4

1. Ethics in Medicine: University of Washington School of Medicine, "Physician-Assisted Suicide," http://eduserv.hscer.washington.edu/bioethics/topics/pas.html.

2. *Hospital Ethics*, May-June 1988, 2.

3. The Death with Dignity Act allows terminally ill Oregon residents to obtain from their physicians and use prescriptions for self-administered, lethal medications. The act states that ending one's life in accordance with the law does not constitute suicide. However, we have used the term "physician-assisted suicide" rather than "Death with Dignity" to describe the provisions of this law because physician-assisted suicide is the term used by the public and by the medical literature to describe ending life through the voluntary self-administration of lethal medications, expressly prescribed by a physician for that purpose. The Death with Dignity Act legalizes physician-assisted suicide but specifically prohibits euthanasia, where a physician or other person directly administers a medication to end another's life. To request a prescription for lethal medications, the Death with Dignity Act requires that a patient must be: (1) an adult (18 years of age or older); (2) a resident of Oregon; (3) capable (defined as able to make and communicate health-care decisions); (4) diagnosed with a terminal illness that will lead to death within six months.

Patients who meet these requirements are eligible to request a prescription for lethal medication from a licensed Oregon physician. To receive a prescription for lethal medication, the following steps must be fulfilled: (1) The patient must make two verbal requests to their physician, separated by at least 15 days. (2) The patient must provide a written request to his or her physician. (3) The prescribing physician and a consulting physician must confirm the diagnosis and prognosis. The prescribing physician and a consulting physician must determine whether the patient is capable. If either physician believes the patient's judgment is impaired by a psychiatric or psychological disorder, such as depression, the patient must be referred for counseling. (4) The prescribing physician must inform the patient of feasible alternatives to assisted suicide, including comfort care, hospice care, and pain control. (5) The prescribing physician must request, but may not require, the patient to notify their next-of-kin of the prescription request.

To comply with the law, physicians must report the writing of all prescriptions for lethal medications to the OHD. Reporting is not required if patients begin the request process but never receive a prescription.

Physicians and patients who adhere to the requirements of the act are protected from criminal prosecution, and the choice of legal physician-assisted suicide cannot affect the status of a patient's health or life insurance policies. Physicians and health-care systems are under no obligation to participate in the Death with Dignity Act <http://www.ohd.hr.state.or.us/cdpe/chs/pas/ar-intro.htm>.

4. Courtney S. Campbell, "Give Me Liberty and Death: Assisted Suicide in Oregon," *Christian Century,* 5 May 1999, 498.

5. Ibid.

6. Patrick McMahon and Wendy Koch, "Oregon Assisted-Suicide Law Is Not Abused, Study Finds," *USA Today,* 24 February 2000, sec. 6A.

7. Derek Humphrey, *Final Exit* (Eugene, Oreg.: Hemlock, 1991).

8. Derek Humphrey, *Let Me Die Before I Wake* (Los Angeles: Hemlock, 1981).

9. Richard A. Marini, "Controversial Pain Relief Bill Wins Support," *Nurse Week/Health Week,* 20 September 1999, www.nurseweek.com/news/99-9/47a.html.

10. *Assisted Suicide and Euthanasia: Christian Moral Perspectives,* produced by Committee on Medical Ethics Episcopal Diocese of Washington, Episcopal Church House, Mount Saint Alban, Washington, DC 20016 (Harrisburg, Pa.: Morehouse Publishing, 1997), 32.

11. Ibid., 23.

12. *Declaration on Euthanasia,* prepared by the Sacred Congregation for the Doctrine of the Faith, Vatican City. 5 May 1980.

13. Campbell, "Give Me Liberty and Death," 498.

14. Peter A. D. Singer, *Practical Ethics* (New York: Cambridge University Press, 1979).

15. Helga Kuhse and Peter Singer, *Should the Baby Live? The Problem of Handicapped Infants* (New York: Oxford University Press, 1985), 138.

16. *Assisted Suicide and Euthanasia,* 36.

17. World Health Organization Technical Report Series 804, "Cancer Pain and Palliative Care" (Geneva: World Health Organization, 1990), 11.

18. An excellent source for information regarding advance directives is "Choice in Dying," http://www.choices.org/. See also http://www.medicareinfo.com/advdirb.html.

19. A 1997 report by *American Health Decisions,* "The Quest to Die with Dignity: An Analysis of Americans' Values, Opinions and Attitudes Concerning End-of-Life Care," is revealing. The report showed that the research participants were skeptical of the current tools for planning their end-of-life care. They viewed documents such as living wills inadequate.

While these Americans insisted that the patient's wishes should always drive treatment decisions, they did not see current advance directives as the answer. Protestants, Catholics, Jews, and Muslims (385 persons) participated in the focus groups from which the conclusions were drawn. *American Health Decisions,* P.O. Box 599, Appleton, WI 54912 (414-832-6670).

Chapter 5

1. Warren Thomas Reich, ed., *Bioethics: Sex, Genetics, and Human Reproduction* (New York: Macmillan, 1995), 455.

2. Ibid., 454.

3. Ibid.

4. *U.S. News & World Report,* 5 October 1998, 66.

5. In fact, according to one study, 97 percent of treatment decisions by doctors are approved by managed-care plans. *Time,* 26 July 1999, 60.

6. Phil Galewitz, "HMOs, Members Saw a Good and Bad Year," *Kansas City Star,* 1 January 2000, sec. C2.

7. *Time,* 22 November 1999, 40.

8. Susan Page, "Uninsured Seniors Charged More for Prescription Drugs," *USA Today,* 10 April 2000.

9. For example, in 1999 Prilosec, used for ulcers and heartburn, cost $99.24 for a bottle of 30 pills in the U.S., $17.14 in Mexico, and $49.53 in Canada. Prozac, used to counter depression, costs $66.41 in the U.S., $28.50 in Mexico, and $22.77 in Canada. Similar discrepancies applied to Lipitor, Prevacid, Zocar, and so forth.

10. In the fall of 1999, Democrats and Republicans introduced into Congress patients' rights bills. Each party charged the other with failure to protect patients. On January 19, 1999, Senate Democratic Leader Tom Daschle introduced in the Senate the *Patients' Bill of Rights.* The bill would guarantee patients greater access to information and necessary care, including access to needed specialists and emergency rooms, guarantees of a fair appeals process when health plans deny care, expanded choice, protection of the doctor-patient relationship, and holding HMOs accountable for decisions that end up harming patients. A companion bill was introduced in the House of Representatives by Congressman John Dingell (D-Michigan). Both bills were supported by President Clinton and a broad coalition of health-care provider groups, patients' rights advocates, medical associations, consumer organizations, and labor.

In January 1999 Senator Don Nickles (R-Oklahoma), Assistant Majority Leader, introduced the Republican *Patients' Bill of Rights Act* (S326). The Democrats immediately attacked the proposal, charging that while the bill appeared to include important patient protections, key provisions were either too weak or missing from the legislation entirely. Opponents of the Democratic measure said that it would result in increasing costs for employers and for employees

On October 7, 1999, Congress did pass a bipartisan managed-care bill that would allow patients to sue their HMOs and PPOs. Some of the bill's most important parts were that it guaranteed the rights of sick patients to see medical specialists and broadened coverage for emergency room care.

One of its most controversial provisions would allow patients to sue their HMOs and PPOs. Commenting on this particular part of the bill, Rep. Merrill Cook (R-Utah) said, "If Americans have the right to sue for a damaged fence or an unsafe toy, they should have the right to sue if their health or life has been endangered or lost. This is a constitutional right. Doctors already face liability, but too often their decisions are forced upon them by an insurance plan. It's only fair, it's only American that the insurance plans be held to the same accountability." Perhaps most remarkable, the House bill represents a bipartisan success. Republican supporters of the bill did so over the objections of the Republican leadership in the House.

The Republican-controlled Senate also passed a health-care bill that would expand consumer rights, but that opposes some of the important parts of the House measure. As the year 2000 began, the two houses had yet to reconcile their differences. Final passage was doubtful. Opponents of tight governmental regulation argued that the market was far ahead of the politicians. Proponents of stiff governmental control say that until HMOs can demonstrate that they can be good citizens, patients will need the protection that comes from the threat of a lawsuit.

11. Since the late 1980s employers have generally shifted more of the cost of health insurance to their employees. Both employers and employees find it increasingly difficult to pay more (Jane Bryant Quinn, "Fighting for Health Care," *Newsweek*, 30 March 1998, 45).

12. Jerry Heaster, "Managed Health Care May Perish," *Kansas City Star*, 26 February 2000, sec. C1. The recent focus has been on Aetna, whose stock price had plunged over the past year. Early in 2000 Aetna reported stronger earnings than Wall Street had anticipated. Aetna's stock should have gone up in value. Instead, the stock continued to decline. As if to punctuate the problem, on February 25, 2000, Aetna shareholders forced the resignation of Richard L. Huber, Aetna's chairman. Shareholders wanted the nation's largest health insurer to boost its ailing stock price and improve its relations with patients and doctors.

13. Froma Harrop, "Our Crazy Health System Needs a Transfusion," *Kansas City Star*, 11 October 1999, sec. B5.

14. Kilner, *Bioethics and the Future of Medicine*, 290.

15. Ibid., 291-95.

16. Beauchamp and Childress, *Principles of Biomedical Ethics*, 351.

17. Ibid., 352.

18. Public health measures, preventive care, primary care, acute care, and special services for those with disabilities.

19. Beauchamp and Childress, *Principles of Biomedical Ethics*, 356.

20. Ibid.

Chapter 6

1. Tim Friend, "Gene Therapy Patient Died of the Procedure, Scientists Determine," *USA Today*, 9 December 1999.

2. The charge was made at a gene-therapy conference at the National Institutes of Health held specifically to discuss Jesse's death.

3. James Chapman, "Tragic Death Carries Message for All Researchers," *Kansas City Star*, 8 January 2000, sec. B8.

4. Peter Gorner, "Fetal Tissue Transplant Opens Up Ethical Quandary," *Chicago Tribune*, 31 January 1997 (Web-posted).

5. Christine Gorman, "Brave New Cells," *Time*, 1 May 2000, 58.

6. Ibid., 59.

7. William C. Mann, "President Panel to Recommend Limited Embryo Research Funding," AP, *Corpus Christi Coller-Times*, 24 May 1999, http://collertimes.com/1999/may/24/today/national/824/html.

8. George E. Will, "Abortionists and Academia," *Kansas City Star*, 20 January 2000, sec. B7.

9. Ruth Ellen Bulger, Elizabeth Meyer Bobby, and Harvey V. Fineberg, eds., *Society's Choices: Social and Ethical Decision Making in Biomedicine* (Washington, D.C.: National Academy Press, 1995), 485-86.

10. "The Inhuman Use of Human Beings: A Statement on Embryo Research by the Ramsey Colloquium," *First Things* 49, January 1995, 17-21.

11. Ibid.

Chapter 7

1. *Kansas City Star*, 8 January 2000, sec. A14.

2. Carol J. Castaneda, "Baby K—Now Stephanie—Turns 2," *USA Today*, 13 October 1994, 3.

3. Shannon, *Introduction to Bioethics*, 159.

4. Alfred N. Whitehead, *The Aims of Education* (New York: Free Press, 1929), 1.

5. Jeff Lyon, *Second Opinion* (Park Ridge, Ill.: Park Ridge Center, 1986), 41.

6. G. Bruce Weir, "How Do We Decide Who Gets Another Chance at Life? Don't Tie Gift of Life to Recipient's Location," *USA Today*, 24 February 1999.

7. Kay Paine, "Shalala Wants to Change Way Organs Distributed," *Amarillo, Texas, Globe News*, 27 February 1998, www.amarillonet.com/stories/022798/shalala.shtml.

8. Ibid.

9. Raanan Gillon, "Transplantation and Ethics," and Robert Schwartz, "Genetic Knowledge: Some Legal and Ethical Questions," in *Birth to Death: Science and Bioethics*, ed. David C. Thomasma and Thomasine Kushner (New York: Cambridge University Press, 1996), 111-12.

10. Gregory K. Pike, "International Trade in Human Organs for Transplant," http://www.bioethics.com/newsc/trade.htm.

11. Gretchen Kell, News Release, Office of Public Affairs, University of California at Berkeley, http://www.urel.berkeley.edu/urel_1/CampusNews/PressReleases/releases/releases.96/14353.html.

Part 4

1. *Splicing Life: The Social and Ethical Issues of Genetic Engineering with Human Beings* (Washington, D.C.: The President's Commission for the

Study of Ethical Problems in Medicine and Bioethical and Behavioral Research, 1982), 2.

2. Ibid., 95.

3. *The Gift of Life (Donum Vitae)*, "Instruction on Respect for Human Life in Its Origin and the Dignity of Procreation," Sacred Congregation for the Doctrine of the Faith, Vatican City, 1987. The document can be read at the following site: www.nccbuscc.org/prolife/tdocs/donumvitae.htm.

4. James Gustafson, *Protestant and Roman Catholic Ethics* (Chicago: University of Chicago Press, 1978).

Chapter 8

1. Tim Friend, "Gattaca Could Foretell Reality," *USA Today*, 28 October 1997.

2. Michael D. Lemonick and Dick Thompson, "Racing to Map Our DNA," *Time*, 11 January 1999, 44-50.

3. "Finding May undo Medical Mysteries," *Kansas City Star*, 1 December 1999, sec. A16.

4. Celera Genomics announced that it had 90 percent of the genome in its database. It had captured 97 percent of all the known human genes and had discovered tens of thousands of new ones. Hundreds of the newly discovered genes included previously unknown neurotransmitter receptors and at least one kind of interferon.

5. Paul Recer, "Milestone in Mapping Human Genome Cited," *Kansas City Star*, 7 April 2000, sec. A1.

6. Recombinant DNA refers to the transfer of a gene from one organism to another, or recombining DNA from different sources. Once the gene is inserted into the DNA of the cell, the cell can be coaxed to express the human gene in preparative amounts. Usually, the protein of interest encoded by the human gene does not exist naturally in quantities required for clinical applications or for biochemical analysis without the use of recombinant DNA technology. The recombinant system is therefore used to produce the protein in high quantities under controlled conditions, thus enabling the researcher to produce large quantities of the purified protein for clinical use.

7. Joyce Tombran-Tink, quoted from correspondence with the author, May 4, 2000.

8. Quoted by Ted Peters, *Playing God? Genetic Determinism and Human Freedom* (New York: Routledge, 1996), 122.

9. Ibid., 125.

10. Ibid., 123.

11. Press Release, November 5, 1998, The Johns Hopkins Medical Institutions Office of Communications and Public Affairs.

12. Michael D. Lemonick, "The Biological Mother Lode," *Time*, 16 November 1998, 96-97.

13. Ibid.

14. The experimentation that led to Dolly was conducted by Ian Wilmut and his colleagues in Edinburgh. They succeeded by taking the nucleus of a mammary gland cell from an adult female sheep and then implanting it in

the unfertilized egg of another animal from which the nucleus had been removed. Previous efforts to use this technique failed because the new nucleus and the recipient egg were unable to synchronize their basic cellular rhythms. Wilmut and colleagues succeeded by making the nucleus of the adult mammary cell stop its normal dividing cycle before being implanted in the egg. Egg cells normally do not divide until fertilized.

15. Jeffrey Kluger, "Cloning the New Babes," *Time*, 27 March 2000, 85.

16. Gerald L. Zelizer "Religious Leaders Rush Too Quickly to Ban Cloning," *USA Today*, 27 July 1998.

17. *Kansas City Star*, 28 April 2000.

18. Ibid., sec. A1.

19. Vanderbilt University Medical Center, Nashville, Tennessee. Gene Therapy, a course taught by David Robertson, M.D., and Jeffery Fritz, Ph.D., http://www.mc.vanderbilt.edu/gcrc/gene/index.html.

20. Ibid.

21. Daniel Callahan, "The Genetic Revolution," in *Birth to Death*, 15.

22. A genetic disorder is a disorder of the fetus caused by a problem with either the genes or the chromosomes. About 3 percent of the babies born in the United States have some type of birth defect. It is estimated that 20 percent of these defects may be genetic. Some genetic disorders can be detected during pregnancy, or in some cases, before pregnancy.

23. Taken from a lecture by Joyce Tombran-Tink at Nazarene Theological Seminary, Kansas City, February 3, 2000.

Chapter 9

1. Laura Parker and Debbie Howlett, "Mom's Multiple 'Miracle': Offers of Help Are Already Coming in for 4 Boys, 3 Girls," *USA Today*, 20 November 1997.

2. Judith Stocks, Ph.D., director of the School of Nursing Education at Northwest Nazarene University, notes that with any multiple pregnancy (even twins), the risks increase. "With each fetus, the risks are greater. The placenta and uterus have limited nutritive ability. The findings with twins now document that many times one twin is malnourished, is much smaller, has more anomalies, and so forth. Yet the public celebrates multiple births as something special when in fact the outcomes are often poor. The child and family are strained forever while dealing with the increased needs. When a chronically ill child drains a family's physical and psychical resources, the rate of divorce is quite high. Christian couples [such as the McCaugheys] can appear to be very selfish as they demand extra measures to conceive three-four fetuses without regard for outcomes" (taken from a letter to the author, April 1, 2000).

3. Of the infertile couples, 25 percent have more than one factor that contributes to their infertility. In approximately 40 percent of infertile couples, the male partner is either the sole cause or a contributing cause of infertility. Tubal blockage and/or peritoneal factors account for approximately 35 percent of all female infertility problems. Irregular or abnormal ovulation accounts for approximately 25 percent of all female infertility cases. Endometriosis is found in about 35 percent of infertile

women who have laparoscopy as part of their infertility workup. Approximately 20 percent of couples who have a complete workup are diagnosed with unexplained infertility because no specific cause can be identified.

4. For example, cervical mucus problems or immunologic factors, a disorder in the immune system.

5. The Infertility Center, http://www.womens-health.com/InfertilityCenter/inf_trt_inseminate.html.

6. J. Bermel, "The Birth of a Feminist Sperm Bank: New Social Agendas for AID," *Hastings Center Report* 13 (February 1983): 3.

7. Joseph G. Schenker and David A. Frenkel, "Medico-Legal Aspects of *In Vitro* Fertilization and Embryo Transfer Practice," *Obstetrical and Gynecological Survey* 41, No. 7, 407.

8. Helmut Thielicke, *The Ethics of Sex*, trans. John W. Doberstein (Grand Rapids: William B. Eerdmans Publishing Co., 1964), 3:259.

9. Paul Ramsey, *Fabricated Man: The Ethics of Genetic Control* (New Haven, Conn.: Yale University Press, 1978), 39, 86.

10. Edward D. Schneider, "Artificial Insemination," in *Questions About the Beginning of Life: Christian Appraisals of Seven Bioethical Issues* (Minneapolis: Augsburg Publishing House, 1985), 27.

11. Thielicke, *Ethics of Sex*, 259.

12. Harmon L. Smith, *Ethics and the New Medicine* (Nashville: Abingdon Press, 1970), 81.

13. The American Surrogacy Center, Inc. (TASC), Marietta, Ga., 1997, www.surrogacy.com.

14. Herbert T. Krimmel, "The Case Against Surrogate Parenting," *The Hastings Center Report* (October 1983), 35.

15. Ibid.

16. The Ethics Committee of the American Fertility Society, *Ethical Considerations of the New Reproductive Technologies* (September 1986), 67.

17. Women's Health Interactive, http://www.womens-health.com/InfertilityCenter/inf_trt_intro.html.

18. Intentionally, the descriptions are clinical, textbook in nature. They do not take into account the many contextual incidences that can complicate the procedures.

19. *U.S. News & World Report*, 12 April 1999, 42-44. The first successful donation occurred in 1984. From that time to April 1999 between 5,000 and 10,000 donor-egg babies had been born. In 1999 alone donor eggs were implanted in more than 5,000 women according to the American Society for Reproductive Medicine. The demand for donor eggs is high because this form of in vitro fertilization is the most successful assisted reproductive technology, particularly for older women. In 1996, 39 percent of egg donations resulted in births, compared with 23 percent when a woman's own eggs are used during in vitro procedures. Because only eggs from young women are used, the success rate doesn't drop when the embryos are transferred to older women. The uterus can support a pregnancy even after menopause. So motherhood via donor egg is viable at almost any age.

With such a high number of couples seeking donor eggs, the law of supply and demand has been triggered. The going rate for compensation is from $2,500 to $5,000. The in vitro procedure adds another $10,000 to $20,000. Not surprisingly, many critics think that the word "donor" is a misnomer. In 1999 an advertisement in a number of high-level universities sought an athletic 5-foot 10-inch egg donor with "1400-plus SAT scores" fueled public alarm not so much because of the desired traits but because the couple offered $50,000 payment. Some clinics are offering what *U.S. News & World Report* calls a "package deal." "Pay for another woman's in vitro fertilization procedure and receive her excess eggs for fertilization." But things can go quite wrong. In April 1999 a Staten Island, New York, couple announced that they would give one of their infant twin boys to a New Jersey couple because the doctor who performed their in vitro fertilizations had mistakenly mingled the two couples' embryos. The second boy is the biological child of the second couple.

20. Leon R. Kass, "Making Babies: The New Biology and the 'Old Morality,'" *Public Interest* 26 (winter 1972), 29-30; as quoted by Paul T. Jersild, "On Having Children: A Theological and Moral Analysis of In Vitro Fertilization," *Questions About the Beginning of Life: Christian Appraisals of Seven Bioethical Issues,* Edward D. Schneider, ed. (Minneapolis: Augsburg Publishing House, 1985), 40. "It is one thing voluntarily to accept the risk of a dangerous procedure for yourself (or to consent on behalf of your child) if the *purpose is therapeutic.* . . . It is quite a different thing to submit a child to hazardous procedures which can in no way be therapeutic for him."

21. Arthur L. Caplan, "The Ethics of In Vitro Fertilization," *Primary Care* 13, No. 2 (June 1986), 241.

22. Favorably comparing the technology of in vitro fertilization to artificial respiration can be called into question. It may be that the analogy between an artificial respirator and in vitro fertilization fails because promoting respiration through the use of technology does not correlate to sexual activity and function. Comparing an artificial respirator to fertilizing ova in a petri dish may be a matter of comparing apples with oranges.

23. Judith Stocks says that against this support there needs to be lodged a warning that while in vitro fertilization may relieve the "suffering" of infertile couples, it may also induce new trauma. Pregnancy through in vitro fertilization may not be as idealized as support describes (letter to the author, April 1, 2000).

24. Taken together, the sperm and egg(s) make up the gamete, the cells that carry the genetic information needed for reproduction.

25. *Kansas City Star,* 25 September 1999, sec. E3.

26. The substance of this description was developed by the American Society for Reproductive Medicine's Ethics Committee and accepted by the Board of Directors on December 8, 1995, http://www.asrm.org, 1209 Montgomery Hwy., Birmingham, AL 35216-2809 (205-978-5000; fax: 205-978-5005; E-mail: asrm@asrm.org).

27. "Monkeys Cloned by Splitting Embryos," *USA Today,* 13 January 1999.

SELECTED BIBLIOGRAPHY FOR FURTHER REFERENCE

I. General and Introductory

Barbour, Ian. *Ethics in an Age of Technology.* San Francisco: Harper Collins, 1993.

Beauchamp, Tom L., and James F. Childress. *Principles of Biomedical Ethics.* 4th ed. New York: Oxford University Press, 1994.

Carney, Thomas P. *Instant Evolution: We'd Better Get Good at It.* Notre Dame, Ind.: University of Notre Dame Press, 1980.

Childress, James F. *Priorities in Biomedical Ethics.* Philadelphia: Westminster Press, 1981.

Coppenger, Mark. *Bioethics: A Casebook.* Old Tappan, N.J.: Prentice-Hall, 1985.

Engelhardt, H. Tristram, Jr. *The Foundations of Bioethics: An Introduction and Critique.* 2nd ed. New York: Oxford University Press, 1996.

Fletcher, Joseph. *Morals and Medicine.* Princeton, N.J.: Princeton University Press, 1954.

Fox, Michael W. *Eating with Conscience: The Bioethics of Food.* Troutdale, Oreg.: NewSage Press, 1997.

Graber, Glenn C., and David C. Thomasma. *Theory and Practice in Medical Ethics.* New York: Crossroad/Continuum, 1992.

Jean, Gabrielle J., ed. *Medical Ethics.* Notre Dame, Ind.: Fides Publishers, 1973.

Howell, Joseph, ed. *Life Choices: A Hastings Center Introduction to Bioethics.* Washington, D.C.: Georgetown University Press, 1995.

Kilner, John F., Nigel M. Cameron, and David L. Shiedermayer. *Bioethics and the Future of Medicine.* Grand Rapids: William B. Eerdmans Publishing Co., 1995.

Nelson, James B. *Human Medicine: Ethical Perspectives on New Medical Issues.* Minneapolis: Augsburg Publishing House, 1983.

Ramsey, Paul. *The Patient as Person.* New Haven: Yale University Press, 1970.

Reich, Warren T., ed. *The Encyclopedia of Bioethics.* 5 vols. London: Simon and Schuster and Prentice-Hall International, 1995.

Shannon, Thomas A. *Bioethics: Basic Writings on the Key Ethical Questions That Surround Modern Biological Possibilities and Problems*. 3rd ed. Mahwah, N.J.: Paulist Press, 1987.

———. *An Introduction to Bioethics*. 3rd ed. Mahwah, N.J.: Paulist Press, 1997.

———. *Law and Bioethics: Selected Cases*. Edited by Jo Ann Manfra. New York: Paulist Press, 1981.

Smith, Harmon L. *Ethics and the New Medicine*. Nashville: Abingdon Press, 1970.

Varga, Andrew C. *Main Issues in Bioethics*. Mahwah, N.J.: Paulist Press, 1984.

Wasserstrom, Richard A., ed. *Today's Moral Problems*. 3rd ed. New York: Macmillan Publishing Co., 1985.

Westerhall, Lotta, and Charles Phillips, eds. *Patient's Rights: Informed Consent, Access and Equality*. Stockholm: Nerenius and Santerus, 1994.

II. Christian Beliefs and Bioethics

Bouma, Hessel, et al. *Christian Faith, Health, and Medical Practice*. Grand Rapids: William B. Eerdmans Publishing Co., 1989.

Episcopal Committee on Medical Ethics, Diocese of Washington. *Assisted Suicide and Euthanasia: Christian Moral Perspectives*. Harrisburg, Pa.: Morehouse Publishing, 1997.

Gill, Robin, Jean Porter, Alastair Campbell, and Paul Badham, eds. *Euthanasia and the Churches: Christian Ethics in Dialogue*. New York: Cassell Academics, 1998. Key Christian ethicists present opposing views on so-called assisted suicide and voluntary euthanasia.

Gustafson, James M. *The Contributions of Theology to Medical Ethics*. Milwaukee, Wis.: Marquette University Press, 1975.

Hauerwas, Stanley. *A Community of Character: Toward a Constructive Social Ethic*. Notre Dame, Ind.: University of Notre Dame Press, 1981.

———. *Suffering Presence: Theological Reflections on Medicine, the Mentally Handicapped and the Church*. Notre Dame, Ind.: University of Notre Dame Press, 1986.

Lammers, Stephen E., ed. *On Moral Medicine: Theological Perspectives in Medical Ethics*. Grand Rapids: William B. Eerdmans Publishing Co., 1998.

Nelson, J. Robert. *Human Life: A Biblical Perspective for Bioethics*. Philadelphia: Fortress Press, 1984.

Schneider, Edward S., ed. *Questions About the Beginning of Life: Christian Appraisals of Seven Bioethical Issues*. Minneapolis: Augsburg Publishing House, 1985.

Shelp, Earl E., ed. *Theology and Bioethics: Exploring the Foundations and Frontiers*. Boston: D. Reidel Publishing Company, 1985.

Wind, James P., ed. *Second Opinion: Health Care, Faith, and Ethics*. Park Ridge, Ill.: Park Ridge Center, 1986.

III. Issues of Life and Death

Battin, Margaret Pabst. *The Least Worst Death: Essays in Bioethics on the End of Life.* New York: Oxford University Press, 1994.

Blank, Robert. *Life, Death, and Public Policy.* Dekalb, Ill: N.I.U. Press, 1988.

Blocher, Mark. *The Right to Die?: Caring Alternatives to Euthanasia.* Chicago: Moody Press, 1999.

Board of Social Responsibility, Church of Scotland. *Abortion in Debate.* Edinburgh: Quorum Press, 1987.

Buchanan, Allen E., and Dan W. Brock. *Deciding for Others: The Ethics of Surrogate Decision Making.* New York: Cambridge University Press, 1989.

Burtchaell, James Tunstead. *Rachel Weeping: The Case Against Abortion.* San Francisco: Harper and Row Publishers, 1982.

Callahan, Daniel. *False Hopes: Why America's Quest for Perfect Health Is a Recipe for Failure.* New York: Simon and Schuster, 1998.

————. *The Troubled Dream of Life: Living with Mortality.* New York: Simon and Schuster, 1991.

————. *What Kind of Life? The Limits of Medical Progress.* Washington, D.C.: Georgetown University Press, 1995.

————, ed. *The World Growing Old: The Coming Health Care Challenges.* Washington, D.C.: Georgetown University Press, 1997.

Callahan, Sidney, and Daniel Callahan. *Abortion: Understanding Differences.* Plenum Publishing Corp., 1984.

Channer, J. H., ed. *Abortion and the Sanctity of Human Life.* Exeter, U.K.: Paternoster Press, 1985.

Cundiff, David. *Euthanasia Is Not the Answer: A Hospice Physician's View.* Totowa, N.J.: Humana Press, 1992.

Feinberg, Joel, ed. *The Problem of Abortion.* 2nd ed. Belmont, Calif.: Wadsworth Publishing Co., 1984.

Gorman, Michael. *Abortion and the Early Church: Christian, Jewish, and Pagan Attitudes.* Downers Grove, Ill: InterVarsity Press, 1982.

Gula, Richard. *Euthanasia: Moral and Pastoral Perspectives.* Mahwah, N.J.: Paulist Press, 1995.

Hackler, Chris, Ray Moseley, and Dorothy E. Vawter. *Advance Directives in Medicine.* Westport, Conn.: Greenwood Publishing Group, 1989.

Hardwig, John. *Is There a Duty to Die?* New York: Routledge Press, 1999.

Hoffmeier, James K., ed. *Abortion: A Christian Understanding and Response.* Grand Rapids: Baker Book House, 1987.

Keown, John, and Daniel Callahan. *Euthanasia Examined: Ethical, Clinical and Legal Perspectives.* New York: Cambridge University Press, 1997.

Larson, Edward J., and Darrel W. Amundsen. *A Different Death: Euthanasia and the Christian Tradition.* Downers Grove, Ill.: InterVarsity Press, 1998.

Lynn, Joanne, ed. *By No Extraordinary Means: The Choice to Forgo Life-Sustaining Food and Water.* Bloomington, Ind.: Indiana University Press, 1989.

Kluge, Eike-Henner W. *The Practice of Death.* New Haven, Conn.: Yale University Press, 1975.

Koop, C. Everett. *The Right to Live; The Right to Die.* Wheaton, Ill.: Tyndale House Publishers, 1976.

Kuhse, Aelga. *The Sanctity-of-Life Doctrine in Medicine.* New York: Clarendon Press, 1987.

Kung, Hans, Walter Jens, Albin Eser, and Dietrich Niethammer. *Dying with Dignity: A Plea for Personal Responsibility.* New York: Continuum Publishing Co., 1996.

Larson, Edward J. and Darrel W. Amundsen. *A Different Death: Euthanasia and the Christian Tradition.* Downers Grove, Ill.: InterVarsity Press, 1999. Surveys the history of euthanasia in Christendom.

Larue, Gerald A. *Euthanasia and Religion: A Survey of the Attitudes of World Religions to the Right-to-Die.* Los Angeles: Hemlock Society, 1985.

Lynn, Joanne, ed. *By No Extraordinary Means: The Choice to Forgo Life-Sustaining Food and Water.* Bloomington, Ind.: Indiana University Press, 1989.

Mace, David R. *Abortion: The Agonizing Decision.* Nashville: Abingdon Press, 1972.

Manipulating Life: Ethical Issues in Genetic Engineering, Church and Society. Geneva: World Council of Churches, 1982.

Manning, Michael. *Euthanasia and Physician-Assisted Suicide: Killing or Caring?* Mahwah, N.J.: Paulist Press, 1999.

McCann, Robert, William Hall, Richard Frankel, Paul Katz, Joshua Chodosh, and Elizabeth Naumberg. *Advance Directives and End of Life Discussions: A Manual for Instructors.* Rochester, N.Y.: University of Rochester, 1997.

McLean, Gary N., ed. *Comprehensive Theological Perspectives on Abortion: A Collection of Manuscripts.* St. Paul: Religious Affairs Committee for Planned Parenthood of Minnesota, 1983.

O'Brien, Linda A. *Advance Directives: Making End of Life Decisions—Resource Guide and Photo Package.* St. Louis: Mosby Year Book, Inc., 1997. Includes a self-directed training package that helps health-care providers discuss end-of-life decisions with their patients and fulfill the mandates of the Self-Determination Act of 1991.

Oden, Thomas C. *Should Treatment Be Terminated?* New York: Harper and Row Publishers, 1976.

Rachels, James. *The End of Life: Euthanasia and Morality.* New York: Oxford University Press, 1986.

Simmons, Paul D. *Birth and Death: Bioethical Decision-Making.* Philadelphia: Westminster Press, 1983.

Singer, Peter. *Rethinking Life and Death: The Collapse of Our Traditional Ethics.* New York: St. Martin's Press, 1994.

Steinbock, Bonnie. *Life Before Birth: The Moral and Legal Status of Embryos and Fetuses.* New York: Oxford University Press, 1992.

Stoddard, Sandol. *The Hospice Movement: A Better Way of Caring.* New York: Vintage, 1992.

Thielicke, Helmut. *The Doctor as Judge of Who Shall Live and Who Shall Die.* Philadelphia: Fortress Press, 1976.

Uhlmann, Michael M., ed. *Last Rights: Assisted Suicide and Euthanasia Debated.* Grand Rapids: William B. Eerdmans Publishing Co., 1997.

Veatch, Robert M. *Case Studies in Medical Ethics.* Cambridge, Mass.: Harvard University Press, 1977.

————. *Life Span: Values and Life-Extending Technologies.* San Francisco: Harper and Row, 1979.

Walter, James J., and Thomas A. Shannon, eds. *Quality of Life: The New Medical Dilemma.* Mahwah, N.J.: Paulist Press, 1990.

Walton, Douglas N. *Ethics of Withdrawal of Life Support Systems: Case Studies in Decision-Making Intensive Care.* Westport, Conn.: Greenwood Publishing Group, 1987.

IV. Human Needs and Technical Resources

Barbour, Ian. *Ethics in an Age of Technology.* San Francisco: HarperSanFrancisco, 1993.

Callahan, Daniel. *Setting Limits: Medical Goals in an Aging Society.* New York: Simon and Schuster, 1987.

Caplan, Arthur L. *If I Were a Rich Man Could I Buy a Pancreas? and Other Essays on the Ethics of Health Care.* Bloomington, Ind.: Indiana University Press, 1992.

Cassell, Eric. *The Nature of Suffering and the Goals of Medicine.* New York: Oxford University Press, 1991.

Durning, A. T. *How Much Is Enough? The Consumer Society and the Future of the Earth.* New York: W. W. Norton and Co., 1992.

Fox, Michael W. *Eating with Conscience: The Bioethics of Food.* Troutdale, Oreg.: NewSage Press, 1997.

Fox, Renee C., and Swazey, Judith. *Spare Parts: Organ Replacement in American Society.* New York: Oxford University Press, 1996.

Zerzan, John, and Alice Carnes, eds. *Questioning Technology: Tool, Toy, or Tyrant?* Santa Cruz, Calif.: New Society Publishers, 1991.

V. Changes in Life at Its Origin

Alpern, Kenneth D., ed. *The Ethics of Reproductive Technology.* New York: Oxford University Press, 1992.

Artificial Insemination, Human. Washington, D.C.: Office of Publishing and Promotion Services, United States Catholic Conference, 1987.

Baruch, Elaine H. *Embryos, Ethics, and Women's Rights: Exploring the New Reproductive Technologies.* Edited by Amadeo F. D'Adamo. New York: Hayworth Press, 1988.

Brannigan, Michael C. *Ethical Issues in Human Cloning.* New York: Seven Bridges Press, 2000.

Burgess, John P. *In Whose Image? Faith, Science, and the New Genetics.* Louisville, Ky.: Westminster/John Knox Press, 1998.

Cole-Turner, Ronald, ed. *Human Cloning: Religious Responses.* Louisville, Ky.: Westminster/John Knox Press, 1998.

Cranor, Carl F., ed. *Are Genes Us? The Social Consequences of the New Genetics.* Piscataway, N.J.: Rutgers University Press, 1994.

Fletcher, Joseph. *The Ethics of Genetic Control: Ending Reproductive Roulette.* Buffalo, N.Y.: Prometheus Books, 1988.

———. *Humanhood: Essays in Biomedical Ethics.* Buffalo, N.Y.: Prometheus Books, 1979.

Glover, Jonathan. *Ethics of New Reproductive Technologies.* DeKalb, Ill.: N.I.U. Press, 1989.

Goodfield, June. *Playing God: Genetic Engineering and the Manipulation of Life.* New York: Harper and Row Publishers, 1977.

Hamilton, Michael P., ed. *The New Genetics and the Future of Man.* Grand Rapids: William B. Eerdmans Publishing Co., 1972.

Haring, Bernard. *Ethics of Manipulation: Issues in Medicine, Behavior Control and Genetics.* New York: Seabury Press, 1975. Intro/Inter.

Howard, Ted, and Jeremy Fitkin. *Who Should Play God? The Artificial Creation of Life and What It Means for the Future of the Human Race.* New York: Dell Publishing Co., 1977.

Jones, D. Gareth. *Brave New People.* "Ethical Issues at the Commencement of Life." Rev. ed. Grand Rapids: William B. Eerdmans Publishing Co., 1985. Intro.

———. *Manufacturing Humans: The Challenge of the New Reproductive Technologies.* England: InterVarsity Press, 1987. Intro.

Karp, Laurence E. *The Ethics of Fetal Research.* New Haven, Conn.: Yale University Press, 1975. Inter.

———. *Genetic Engineering: Threat or Promise?* Chicago: Nelson-Hall, 1976. Inter.

Kevles, Daniel J., and Leroy Hood, eds. *Scientific and Social Issues in the Human Genome Project.* Cambridge, Mass.: Harvard University Press, 1992.

Kilner, John F., Rebecca D. Pentz, and Frank E. Young, eds. *Genetic Ethics: Do the Ends Justify the Genes?* Grand Rapids: William B. Eerdmans Publishing Co., 1997.

Lauritzen, Paul. *Pursuing Parenthood: Ethical Issues in Assisted Reproduction.* Bloomington, Ind.: Indiana University Press, 1993.

Overall, Christine. *Human Reproduction: Principles, Practices, Policies.* New York: Oxford University Press, 1993.

Peters, Ted. *Playing God: Genetic Determinism and Human Freedom.* New York: Routledge, 1999.

Ramsey, Paul. *Fabricated Man: The Ethics of Genetic Control.* New Haven, Conn.: Yale University Press, 1970.

Regan, Tom. *The Case for Animal Rights.* Berkeley, Calif.: University of California Press, 1983.

Robertson, John A. *Children of Choice: Freedom and the New Reproductive Technologies.* Princeton, N.J.: Princeton University Press, 1994.

Shannon, Thomas. *Surrogate Motherhood.* New York: Crossroad, 1988.

———. *What Are They Saying About Genetic Engineering?* New York: Paulist Press, 1987.

DATE DUE

NOV 1 8 2016			

S.A.

33710001253363
Truesdale, Albert,
God in the laboratory : equipping
Christians to deal with issues in
bioethics /
W 50 .T78 2000